82-

Detoxification
and Healing

Detoxification
and Healing

Completely Revised and Up-to-Date

The Key to Optimal Health

Sidney MacDonald Baker, M.D.

Contemporary Books

Chicago   New York   San Francisco   Lisbon   London   Madrid   Mexico City
Milan   New Delhi   San Juan   Seoul   Singapore   Sydney   Toronto

The *McGraw-Hill* Companies

Library of Congress Cataloging-in-Publication Data

Baker, Sidney M.
    Detoxification and healing : the key to optimal health / Sidney MacDonald
Baker.—Rev. ed.
        p.   cm.
    Previous ed. published under title: Detoxification & healing.
    Includes bibliographical references and index.
    ISBN 0-658-01219-3
    1. Detoxification (Health)   I. Detoxification & healing.   II. Title.

    RA784.5.B35   2003
    613—dc21   2003055226

2 3 4 5 6 7 8 9 0   DOC/DOC   0 9 8 7 6 5 4

ISBN 0-658-01219-3

Interior design by Rattray Design

McGraw-Hill books are available at special quantity discounts to use as premiums and
sales promotions, or for use in corporate training programs. For more information, please
write to the Director of Special Sales, Professional Publishing, McGraw-Hill, Two Penn
Plaza, New York, NY 10121-2298. Or contact your local bookstore.

Detoxification and Healing is not intended as medical advice. Its intention is solely
informational and educational. Please consult a medical or health professional should the
need for one be indicated. The information in this book lends itself to self-help. For
obvious reasons, the author and publisher cannot take the medical or legal responsibility
of having the contents herein considered as a prescription for everyone. Either you, or the
physician who examines and treats you, must take the responsibility for the uses made of
this book.

This book is printed on acid-free paper.

For my wife, Louise

Contents

Acknowledgments

THE IDEAS AND facts presented in this book are not mine but come from various teachers, of whom my patients have been the best. The first, however, was Richard Mayo-Smith, my biology teacher at Phillips Exeter Academy, who rescued me from the illusion that science was all math and facts. He introduced me to the notion of ideas: that what we make of the facts depends on our ability to conceive of a framework in which to see the facts.

The late Linus Pauling based his perceptions about the molecular basis for treatment of illness on two very simple ideas: 1. everyone is different, and 2. each individual's health benefits from having "the right molecules in the right amounts." His lectures in courses given for physicians at Stanford inspired me to follow medical paths that obey these two precepts, which Dr. Pauling called "orthomolecular medicine" (meaning the "right molecules medicine"). The medical profession's rejection of his notions made it professionally risky to identify oneself as a doctor with orthomolecular leanings. However, a growing number of health professionals are joining the many laypeople who believe that before turning to medications we should attempt to adjust the normal body constituents to match needs for optimal functioning. I hope that a recognition of the orthomolecular implications of much of the current literature in nutritional medicine will lead to a renewed acceptance of orthomolecular medicine.

My friend, Leo Galland, M.D., and I worked together in the 1980s. Then and now Leo was a source of ideas and information that have been essential to the foundations of this book.

Another student of Dr. Pauling, Dr. Jeffrey Bland, has been the most influential teacher of physicians in the past three decades. Like many of my colleagues who set out to relearn biochemistry long after passing Part I Board Exams at the end of the second year of medical school, I owe him my ongoing thanks for his thoughtful and encyclopedic sifting of the current medical literature. I also owe special thanks to Dr. Jon Pangborn of Bionostics Laboratories, West Chicago, Illinois. Thirty years ago Jon set out to turn his knowledge of biochemistry into useful tools for gaining insight into individual biochemistry. Since then he has invested enormous amounts of time, energy, and his impeccable integrity for the benefit of doctors and their patients who are looking for the biochemical basis of chronic health problems.

Other teachers and colleagues whose influence and ideas appear in this book are Drs. Karl Ernst Schaefer, Otto Wolff, Theron Randolph, Joe Beasley, Clyde Hawley, Phyllis Saifer, Larry Dickey, Frank Waickman, William Rea, Martin Lee, Stephen Barrie, John Rebello, James Braly, Orian Truss, Paul Cheney, Lloyd Saberski, William Crook, Leonard McEwen, Charles L. Remington, and my friend Colin Furness whose friendship and advice have helped illuminate the path that made writing this book possible.

My most consistent teachers have been my patients. The lessons of a few of them are told in this book. Hundreds of others have helped shape me as a physician as I developed the skills of explaining things that I have used in writing this book. The even more important skills of listening, listening again, and going over the story yet another time in the quest for clues to clinical puzzles are not so clearly evident in the chapters of this book in which I have chosen relatively simple cases. Becoming a good listener has been my principal aim as I have learned to respect the deep knowledge and intuition that my patients have about their bodies. What they lack is a scientific vocabulary, so that their initial efforts to explain their perceptions about their illness and its causes offend a scientific ear that has not been tuned to hear the signal through the noise.

My clinical assistants over the past thirty-five years have contributed their own listening skills to mine and helped create the time and space and atmosphere for listening in my office. They have been Jayne Barese, RN; Gail Sherry, RN; Lisa Young, RMA; Holly Pommer; Veronica Brown, RMA; Dell Lamoureux, LPN; Maureen McDonnell, RN; and Nancy Miller, RN.

My special thanks go to my brother, David E. Baker, whose enduring love and support have added to the strength needed to complete many of the tasks I have undertaken. To my daughters, Jennifer and Laura, I will always be grateful for their loyal love and forbearance during the time I have taken out to write.

I never sit for long at the keyboard without feeling the inspiration of my main model for writing, Louise Bates Ames, Ph.D., cofounder of the Gesell Institute and my friend and mentor since the time I worked with her there. The staccato of her typewriter was the music heard up and down the stairs of the old Victorian mansion on Prospect Street from 1950 until her death at age eighty-eight in October 1996. No one in my life has provided for me a better model for candor, wit, persistence, and value placed on the practical application of scientific insight.

Thanks to Drs. Louis Magnardli, John Anderson, and Bill Kriski for their answers to my questions concerning toxic ticks.

I am very grateful to Karen Baar, MPH, who helped me edit this revision and contributed material and advice on its new structure.

Preface

IT TAKES ABOUT twenty-five years for a new idea to catch on in medicine. That is the time required for it to be tested in the crucible of science and become accepted as official policy. For example, there was sufficient information available in 1975[1] for a young woman to assume that taking a supplement of the B vitamin folic acid in pregnancy would prevent certain severe birth defects in her child. During the two decades it has taken for the folic acid connection to birth defects to be proven, thousands of babies have been born who might have been spared serious defects if their mothers had been able to make a personal choice based on their reading of the research instead of waiting for folic acid supplementation to become public policy. I am talking about ideas, not drugs, devices, or procedures, although they have a similar time line from emergence to acceptance. This book will help you grasp current ideas and watch them catch on. You may want to accept these ideas as they apply to your personal health well before they have achieved the cachet of official acceptance. You may also want to consider many of the ideas in this book that will never be subjected to the rigorous and expensive processes needed to prove their validity.

Integrative medicine is the application of the kind of thinking embodied in general systems theory to medicine. Integrative medicine has mostly to do with the approach one takes to understanding what has caused an event, such as a symptom or the collection of symptoms, signs, and lab tests we call an illness. At present, medical thinking remains quite linear and simple. Doctors and patients alike are tempted by the idea that an illness has a single cause that can be treated with a single pill. General systems theory presents ideas about causality in which a web of interactions produces a result that is not as easy to blame on a single factor. Health is sustained by a state of balance among countless strands of a web of genetic, physiologic, psychological, developmental, and environmental factors. When something goes wrong, it makes sense to pay attention to all aspects of this web that can be addressed with reasonable cost and risk. The occasional reference to integrative medicine in this book is a shorthand for the application of the principles of general systems theory to medicine.

There are two meanings of the word *systems*. When I became a doctor I learned about systems as a way of dividing the body and categorizing diseases that affect it. There are the cardiovascular, nervous, immune, reproductive, gastrointestinal, urinary, integumentary (skin), musculoskeletal, endocrine, reticuloendothelial, and hematologic systems. In my medical training all my textbooks and all my courses were organized according to these divisions of the body. The same systems are the basis for classifying disease. When I graduated from medical school I was expected to pick a system and become a specialist. I could not decide on my favorite system. I did some training in obstetrics and completed my training in pediatrics to help me understand human development. I have remained a generalist and still stumble when the person in the next seat on an airplane asks me what kind of doctor I am.

I finished my specialty training in pediatrics in 1969 and, rather than taking a fellowship in heart, kidney, or liver, I spent two years as the junior member in the new section of Medical Computer Science at Yale Medical School. Dean Fritz Redlich had conceived the idea of a computer section devoted not to number crunching but to finding ways to make computers useful in the day-to-day practice of medicine. My mentor was Dr. Shannon Brunjes, who began his academic career by specializing in the adrenal gland. His research entailed the use of computers. From Shannon I learned about systems theory in which the notion of system is quite different from the accepted medical way of dividing the body. Systems theory provides a unifying, as opposed to divisive, concept of how things work in nature as well as in computers. It allowed me to view biological systems as unified by the interaction of their many components and to make functional, as opposed to anatomical divisions, as I assessed balance within the whole system.

The medical concept of systems and disease leads a doctor toward a narrow path. The student doctor learns to take pride in a parsimonious approach to finding the one explanation for the patient's problem. The doctor gives the diagnosis, the name of the disease, as the explanation of the patient's problem and is comfortable saying that the disease is the cause of the symptoms. "Your sadness is being caused by depression," "Your high blood pressure is the result of hypertension," "Your cramps and diarrhea are being caused by colitis," "Your child can't pay attention because he has attention deficit disorder." Having made the diagnosis, the doctor may then apply the treatment that works best for that symptom: an antidepressant for depression, an antihypertensive for hypertension, a pill to suppress cramps and diarrhea, or Ritalin for the hyperactive child, a drug that would lead to the imprisonment of anyone found selling it near the playground.

Doctors who adhere to the emerging concepts of systems theory follow a broad path. Students of this approach take pride in a lavish approach that considers all the components of the patient's system that might be out of balance. The doctor makes a functional assessment with the understanding that the diagnosis is the name, not the cause, of the patient's symptoms. Having made the diagnosis, the doctor makes a functional assessment of the *individual* patient's balance and prescribes the supplementation of needed elements and the removal of toxic elements that interfere with balance. The broad path is less costly in the long run because it is faithful to the realities of the interrelationships in biological systems.

In 1959 I was a premed student just finished with nine months of traveling and studying Asian art history with my teacher Nelson Wu, when I went to work with Dr. Edgar Miller in Kathmandu, Nepal, for three months before returning to my senior year at Yale. I had the privilege of being Dr. Miller's sidekick and assistant when he saw patients as part of his affiliation with Shanta Bhawan, a missionary hospital that, in the 1950s, represented the first presence of outsiders in the

Kingdom of Nepal. Dr. Miller had retired at age sixty-five from his cardiology practice in Wilmington, Delaware, and, with his wife, Elizabeth, a pediatrician, had joined the staff of what was then the only well-staffed, well-equipped medical facility in the valley of Kathmandu. In weekly clinics in outlying villages we saw patients who would line up at dawn to wait for Dr. Miller and his small team of Nepalese helpers and me. In spite of the dust, the heat, the crowded quarters provided on the second story of a village dwelling, and the pressure to see every patient and return to Kathmandu the same day, Dr. Miller would turn to me after assessing each patient and ask, "Sidney, have we done everything we can for this patient?" I can hear the sound of his voice as I write these words and as I could all through my medical training when none of my other teachers ever posed such a question in such a way.

Dr. Miller's question takes on a different significance for a generalist and a systems analyst than it does for a specialist, a person focusing on one particular system. It is not just a question of the generalist concentrating on a large territory and the specialist on a restricted one. It is the kind of question that goes with systems theory as applied to medicine versus the present model in medicine that views the disease, not the individual, as the target of treatment. If I look at a patient and ask myself Dr. Miller's question, it makes all the difference in my approach to that patient's problem. If I view the patient as a complex system interacting with the environment, the difference is that I must do everything reasonable to help establish balance in the system.

Balance means providing all the necessary elements to optimize the system and removing any interfering elements. Nutrients are necessary elements. Toxins are interfering elements. The difficulty is that each of us is unique, and the necessary and interfering elements differ, sometimes widely, from person to person. In systems analysis, in treating each person as a unique problem, what counts are the differences between that person and others. In traditional medicine, in treating each person as a disease, it is the similarities that count. As I am defining it, integrative medicine means understanding health as an ever-shifting state in the complex web of interactions which, when working in harmony, yield a dynamic balance that we experience as feeling well.

As is true for computers, integrative medicine in biology can be grasped, even by the beginner, in terms of such certain recurring generalized functions as input, storage, and output for a computer, and perception, memory, and language for a person.

When I finished my training and thought I could stamp out illness with my ballpoint pen and prescription pad, I was comfortable with the landmarks I had been given to find my way as a doctor. I had a detailed view of the real world inside the human body as well as an imaginary world populated by diseases whose attack I believed to be responsible for illness. A belief in that imaginary world works quite well in the management of the acute illness that one encounters in hospital wards where most medical training takes place, and the narrow path works quite well for treating trauma, acute infections, or the intense phase of a psychosis. Belief in the same imaginary world did not work well for me as I entered family practice in a health maintenance organization, and patients began asking me questions that began with the word *could*: "Could my cramps and diarrhea be caused, not by colitis, but by something I am eating?" "Could taking vitamins help my depression?" "Could my child's hyperactivity be caused by allergies?" As I began to struggle with the answers to those questions in the spirit of Dr. Miller's question, "Have I done everything I can for this patient?" I began to leave the security of the narrow path, putting a tentative foot on the broad path of the systems approach to health. The first ten chapters of this book tell the stories of patients who have helped me find security on the broad path.

As I have tried to sort out my patients' chronic illnesses over thirty-five years of practice, I have found a much more navigable and realistic terrain than the imaginary one I learned in medical school in which illness is seen as the attack of a disease. The landscape of integrative medicine* is revealed in a functional, as opposed to an anatomical, view of things. Of all the various functions in human biology there is one overriding function that connects to all the others. Understanding its chemistry and immunology can unify the physician's approach to problems of any level of complexity. It is detoxification.

---

*See Baker, S. M. The medicine we are evolving. *Integrative Medicine*, vol. 1, no. 1 (December 2002/January 2003).

When I speak of detoxification, I do not mean a treatment for alcohol and drug abuse, although such treatments are tangentially related to the subject of this book. I mean the processes by which the body rids itself of unwanted materials. I do not mean what happens in the bathroom, whether that is bathing or emptying the bowels or bladder. I refer to the biochemistry of handling potentially harmful chemicals that appear within the system and must be neutralized before they pass from the body. I am not referring exclusively to the harmful environmental chemicals we have all learned to fear: lead, mercury, other heavy metals, additives, dyes, hormones, pesticides, herbicides, fungicides, and petrochemicals of all sorts or pollutants of the air, water, and food supply that we ingest.

Detoxification is central to understanding functional assessment in medicine not so much because we live in a toxic environment but because detoxification is the biggest item in each individual's biochemical budget. It handles waste not only from the environment, but from every process in all the organs and systems of the body. Nearly every molecule the body handles has to be gotten rid of when it has served its purpose. Doing so involves a deliberate process of rendering the molecule inactive. It is a synthetic activity, a creative enterprise in which small molecules—such as the ammonia left over from protein metabolism, hormones no longer needed by the endocrine system, used neurotransmitters from the nervous system, or the by-products of a well-functioning immune system—must be changed before they can be safely excreted from the body.

Illness and disease will affect the body's detoxification chemistry, and if there is something wrong with the detoxification chemistry, any other problems will be aggravated. It is central to all systems. Detoxification chemistry provides the map and the vehicle for understanding the functional landscape of each human being. It offers a new way to defend the body's health by establishing and maintaining a state of balance instead of waiting in fear for an expensive disease to strike. In fact, the conventional medical disease-oriented approach to health care is sinking the medical economy. We will not be able to save medical dollars until we change the way we think about illness.

You need not wait for public policy to recover from the collapse of the current health-care system to adopt practices based on a modern understanding of biologic systems. If you understand some basic principles, you can make choices that will reduce your risk of illness and enhance your health. In the chapters that follow, I will retrace some of the paths I have taken as a practicing physician. Then I will explore how the chemistry and immunology of detoxification unifies our grasp on health problems more effectively than just giving problems a name and prescribing pills to suppress symptoms. I will explain detoxification chemistry and the tests that can be used to investigate how yours works. The concept of toxin embraces a wide variety of familiar substances that may pose problems for some people and not others. Individuality is the key to this book. Taking charge of your own health depends on knowing how to assess your individual biochemical and immunologic quirks. This book is designed to help you by using the same method I use in my office, taking plenty of time to explain detoxification concepts and considering all the angles.

This book is a personal account. The practice of medicine is a very personal activity in which I take responsibility for sifting and filtering scientific information for my patients just as I have done in writing this book. This is not a dispassionate and objective overview of biochemistry, nutrition, detoxification, or any other branch of objective science. The older I get, the more convinced I am that much of science depends on personal viewpoints, if not on personalities. In these pages you will find facts and ideas that are not all mine, but their assembly is a reflection of my personal viewpoint as a practicing physician.

This revision of *Detoxification and Healing* adds dos and don'ts to the whys and wherefores of the first edition. The added prescriptive information will make it easier when you come to saying "OK, I get the point, but give me some simple steps I can do." Understanding the ideas that underlie the dos and don'ts will, I hope, keep the simple steps from being simpleminded. You may wish to turn to the last chapter of the book for a summary of some ideas that I have just mentioned and others that lie ahead in your reading of this book.

1

The Unity of the Immune System and Central Nervous System

IN EXPLAINING TO my patients how I go about the detective work involved in unraveling their problems, I sometimes recite the "Tacks Rules" to make my point.

1. If you are sitting on a tack, it takes a lot of aspirin to make it feel good.
2. If you are sitting on two tacks, removing just one does not result in a 50 percent improvement.

Let's look at the first rule. You could substitute the word *aspirin* with *psychotherapy*, *meditation*, *organic foods*, or *vitamins* and the rule still applies: the proper treatment for tack-sitting is tack removal. Get at the root of the matter and fix it. In particular, don't take medicine to cover up a symptom instead of looking for the cause.

Chronic illness has two common roots, one of which is illustrated by the first rule: the body may be irritated by an unwanted substance. If not a tack, it could be a disagreeable substance such as a food that causes an allergy; it could be lead or a germ or a naturally occurring or manufactured toxin. The presence of some unwanted substance is a common root of illness.

The second rule helps explain what I mean by root. Becoming chronically ill usually results from a combination of factors. It is unrealistic to think in terms of a single cause when several factors inevitably contribute to a problem. It is especially unrealistic to recommend a single treatment to remedy a complex chronic illness when several factors deserve attention. The factors may have to do with the presence of an unwanted substance or the lack of a needed substance. The main focus of this book is ridding one's body of unwanted substances, that is, detoxification. As you will see, effective detoxification cannot work well without critical dietary substances. Complete avoidance of offending allergens or toxins is not usually possible. Good nutrition to supply individual needs for certain basic nutrients becomes a top priority in improving efficient detoxification mechanisms. The basic biochemical facts of detoxification are well established. My job is to enable you to make sense of the facts, many of which you already know.

Look at yourself. Do you see any part of yourself that is the same as it was when you were a baby? No. You are different. Is there anywhere in your body where you can find a cell that is the identical, undivided cell present when you were first old enough to blow out some candles on your birthday cake? Before trying to answer that question, let me pose a related question: if you think back to your first remembered birthday, where did you put that memory so that it still evokes the candles, the cake, your playmates, or some extraneous detail of the day? You did not put the memory in your fingernails, or your hair, or skin, or liver, or heart. All the cells of such parts have long since been replaced. Granted, each cell transmits a certain kind of memory to its progeny when it divides, but that memory does not have to do with birthday parties, it has to do with your ancestors. Each cell carries DNA encoding your ancestral memory. But each cell does not have encoded pictures of your little friend Jeffrey spilling fruit punch all over himself and your new sneakers when you turned seven.

There are only two places in your body where there are cells which have remained undivided and unchanged except for aging. One place is your brain, where there are many cells that do not replace themselves, but remain intact from infancy until death. The other place is the immune system, comprised mainly of certain kinds of cells, called lymphocytes, which are spread widely throughout the body with certain strategic concentrations. Lymphocytes of the immune system arise from parent cells and then go on to live a life of days to months. There is a subset of lymphocytes that arises in the early stages of development from the same source as brain cells and, like certain brain cells, remain the undividing guardians of the persistence and the memory of our self. Look at yourself again. It is not obvious that your body contains two sets of permanent cells in your brain and immune system, nor is it obvious that your body is made up of cells. It is: 100,000,000,000,000 (100 trillion) of them. Life goes on in the cells. Each cell is a unit of life. All of the processes that you will contemplate in reading this book take place inside of cells or on the surfaces of cells within your body. You may remember hearing that cells multiply. It seems quite reasonable that a number as big as 100 trillion must be the product of multiplication. Not so. All cells come into being as the result of *division*: division of the first cell from which each of us originally derived. That cell, the fertilized egg, was lost as it divided into two cells, which each in turn divided into two, which each in turn divided into two, and so on. But the continuing process of division does not go on indefinitely. As you developed, certain cells took on specialized functions: the capacity to remain as nerve cells or lymphocytes, which are the guardians of your essential self.

From the time the permanent cells established themselves during the early months of your existence, all of the other cells of your body became, by comparison, relatively transient. Blood cells live three to four months. That is an intermediate life span between the short-lived cells of the surface of your tongue, subject to daily wear and tear and replacement, and the cells of your bones and other deep structures, that are replaced at a more leisurely pace. Whether it is sooner or later, however, the dying of each transient cell is the end of a life of service to the small minority of enduring and immutable cells.

Most of us have an instinct to protect our permanent brain cells, which, after all, have the conspicuous protection of our skull. We know that harm to these cells presents a completely different problem than, say, a broken bone or a tongue burned on a hot cup of tea.

We do not have the same instinct to protect our permanent lymphocytes. We are not directly conscious of their doings, and they are not as subject to the sort of collective slaughter that occurs with serious trauma or loss of blood supply as, say, in a stroke. If you become aware of the need to protect the health of your permanent cells, then you will need to learn ways to keep the cells as fresh and flexible as possible.

Caring for the transient cells of the body is also important. Cancer or the failure of a vital organ can arise in these cells and the injured cells often cannot simply be replaced. However, certain cells of the central nervous system and the immune system share at least one key attribute: an enduring presence in each of us from infancy to old age.

There are other features shared by the central nervous system and the immune system. The first such shared feature is memory. Memory depends on the persistence of permanent nerve and immune cells. It does not seem that brain memories are inside individual brain cells, so you won't lose the recollection of your seventh birthday party or the candles or the cake with the loss of a particular cell. However, the capacity for memory resides exclusively in the two tissues of the body where the permanent cells reside, linking these two features (permanence of cells and the capacity for memory) in the brain and immune system. Another feature of both systems is perception. Without perceiving the world, there would be nothing to remember. The brain perceives the world with the senses: vision, hearing, taste, smell, and touch.

Look at yourself yet a third time. You are perforated. You have a pair of eyes, ears, nostrils, and a mouth by which you take in the world. Eating involves a very literal taking in of the edible parts of the world, but otherwise I speak of "taking in" the world of our senses when I perceive a friend's face in a photo on the wall of my office, the chirping of the chipmunks waiting for me to feed the birds, the scent of the garden, or the feel of the keyboard as I write these words. The face, the sounds, the peonies and roses, and the keys that I perceive this morning have been taken in without actually entering me. Their images have come to share residence in my enduring nerve cells, my central nervous system.

For example, while I was taking in the morning air I was also taking in something of which I was unaware until a sudden chain of sneezes left me incapable of attending to anything beyond the tip of my busy nose. What was that all about? It was a response to having taken in something that I did not notice with my conscious mind. Grass pollen grains on the morning breeze found their way to the mucous membranes of my nose where they were perceived not by my brain's senses but by my immune system. My immune system has remembered something disagreeable about grass pollen and was able to pick up the offensive taste or smell of it while my brain was happily focusing on the peonies and roses and completely unaware of the grass pollen. Then my chain of sneezes let me know that my old antagonist was getting to me. Without my conscious participation, my immune system has noticed and responded to particles that would otherwise be visible only to the eye aided by a microscope. My immune system has done something fully equivalent to the activity of my senses and my brain working together: recognition.

The main difference between the activity of my immune system with respect to the grass pollen and my brain with respect to the everyday world of my senses is a matter of scale. My senses and brain take in and remember, hence recognize, the big world of faces, peonies, roses, chipmunks, and keyboards. My immune recognition deals with the invisibly small world of pollens, molds, germs, and molecules. The chemistry of immune recognition is actually a lot like the chemistry of perceiving odors, and the chemistry of the immune system in general shares many of the molecules that carry out central nervous system function. Whether you smell something or your immune system identifies it, what happens at the level of cells and molecules is about the same. The main difference is that hearing, seeing, or touching enriches the experience of odor so that you can build a conscious experience of recognizing various foods, flowers, perfumes, or unpleasant odors. Even so, we don't have a rich vocabulary of words describing odors and a good deal of our behavior is modified by unconscious responses to odors we detect. Even odors we do not detect consciously may have a big effect on our behavior. When your immune system detects something, the process is very much like such an unconscious effect of an odor. It all happens, so to speak, beneath the radar of your central nervous system, but it is still a kind of perception that sets your chemistry in motion. So far I have made the point that memory resides in the central nervous and immune systems, which are the home of the body's permanent cells. Now I am saying that the brain and immune system share another function: perceiving the world.

When we perceive things in the world of our senses, we are used to combining input from more than one sense to get the full picture of what is going on around us. We have a direct experience of the combined use of our senses. We do not need scientists to tell us that my experience of this morning's walk has required an overlapping, redundant collaboration of my vision, hearing, olfactory sense, and touch to get me to my cottage. We do need scientists to tell us how the immune system carries out a similar overlapping, redundant collaboration of its perceptual faculties to form a picture of what is going on, not so much around, but in, me. At its current state of development, immunology tends to view immune perception and memory in its particulars rather than in its combined effects. Major debates go on among scientists who have invested generous measures of ego in the importance of a particular immune mechanism in the detection of my offending grass pollen. My guess is that when it is all better understood, we will find that the immune system works very much like our senses and brain with respect to the combined, redundant, and overlapping efforts of various "senses" required to identify and respond to our microscopic and molecular world.

Immune function and central nervous function are identical. Each perceives and each remembers. We use the word *recognition* with equal comfort in describing activities (perception and memory) shared by the brain and immune system. The only difference, except for anatomy, is the size of the objects we perceive and remember.

The only event I now remember from the first week of September 1960, when I first entered medical school, was my introduction to the corpse of a woman who had generously donated her body for my instruction. I cannot remember the location of my mailbox, my lecture room in public health, statistics, or physiology, or where I parked my car, but I remember every muscle, nerve, and artery of the cadaver I shared with my classmate, Richard V. Lee. I remember the smell and the layout of the room, the location of our dissecting table by the door, and the gradual revealing of the tissues' mysteries as I dissected day by day for nine months.

As I learned anatomy I also learned that my activities were part of a tradition that began during the Renaissance when medical scientists began the methodical dissection of cadavers. The arrangement and appearance of the internal organs, and later, their appearance under a microscope, formed the basis for understanding the workings of the body. Physicians who based their practice on such an understanding could claim a justifiable expertise gained from being able to visualize things that are ordinarily invisible.

Like pioneer anatomists and surgeons and like every other initiate medical student I tried to learn how the body works by exploring its details. My microscope took me beyond the sight and feel of the embalmed tissues. I saw how strikingly different the cells that form the tissue of the various organs appeared under the microscope. Muscle cells are long and slender, skin cells are flat like flagstones, cells that line the bowel wall are gobletlike cylinders, and nerve cells have extensions so long that it takes only two cells to connect the brain and toes. It took a special insight for early histologists to realize that, however different, all tissues were divisible into the same basic subunit: the cell. The fantastic differences between the shapes of cells correspond to their varying functions. From that perspective, the cells of the brain, with their long roots and branches, all consolidated in the head, seem quite alien to the cells of the immune system with their individually compact appearance and collectively scattered distribution in the body. It is understandable that the unity of the immune system and the central nervous system might be overlooked by anyone penetrating the body's mysteries with a dissecting scalpel, probe, and microscope.

The medical sciences of non-European cultures did not rely on dissection as a way of penetrating the inner workings of the body. An accumulation of empirical evidence based on the testimony of living, not dead, bodies gave rise to an "anatomy" that seems quaint because its diagrams do not fulfill the eye's expectations based on surgery and dissection of cadavers. The diagrams may, however, present a picture of the dynamic balance among forces inside and outside the body that cannot be perceived in a cadaver. Neither European traditions of anatomical dissection nor non-European empirical and contemplative traditions recognized the key notion that the immune system and central nervous system are in fact unified.

The immune system was the only part of my cadaver that I could not localize. I found the spleen, the remnants of a thymus gland beneath the breastbone, lots of insignificant appearing lymph nodes, and the place deep in the left side of the neck where the entire lacy network of the body's lymphatic vessels drains through a single passage into the subclavian ("under the collarbone") vein. Only in the last three generations have scientists understood how this system works at a cellular and molecular level, and only fifteen years ago did I first hear a professor of immunology (John Dwyer at Yale) state that the immune system and central nervous system share the distinction of being homes for cells that remain intact from infancy to old age. He and I and others of our generation in medicine, and you, perhaps, are startled to think that the immune system and the brain are really the same system. We have been schooled to think anatomically that these domains are quite separate. A "new discipline" of psychoneuroimmunology has grown up around observations linking the function of the brain and psyche with that of the immune system, which had been considered on anatomical grounds to be quite separate. For example, many individuals who have suffered the loss of a loved one undergo a period of immune suppression during the time of their most intense grief. As startling as the connections between the brain and immune system may be for those of us who have based our thinking on anatomy, we should not be surprised to recognize the immune system and brain as a unit if we base our thinking on function.

Fran White was a thirty-seven-year-old married mother of two. When she came to me, she described how she had become gradually more and more sensitive to foods, chemicals, pollens, molds, dust, and animals. She had consulted several allergists, who either confirmed that she indeed had positive test reactions to numerous substances or told her that she represented a therapeutic challenge because she was sensitive to everything.

As we talked, two forces pulled me toward what turned out to be a key part of my initial interview with her. One was my routine attempt to be consistent and thorough and to touch all the bases. Another was more intuitive, based on her response when I explained the unity of the immune system and the central nervous system. I illustrated my point by saying that sometimes bad experiences, or invasive life events that hurt your feelings, can be buried in ways that make trouble for your immune system. Examples of such occurrences are an unfortunate experience with a tonsillectomy or another invasive medical procedure, a lack of personal privacy during development, and, especially, problems associated with sexual molestation and abuse. Her eyes welled up as she said, "I have never told anyone this before, but my uncle molested me from the time I was nine to the time I was twelve."

This important landmark in her emotional landscape did not turn out to be the sole cause of her sensitivities. Her mom had asthma and her brother had hay fever, so there were some genetic factors in place. She also had recurring yeast infections, which can shift the immune system toward being more sensitive. I believe, however, that her invasive life experiences played a key role. Fran had buried her anger against her uncle and her family as well as her misplaced anger toward herself. That anger, not finding an outlet, burrowed into her soul and her immune system to create a basis for her hypervigilance. Of course, she was not hypervigilant in the same sense that I was after being mugged on a dark street one night—thereafter, I walked down the street with a much more attentive eye for danger. Her hypervigilance was expressed in the way her immune system responded to her environment.

Taking a fresh look at human beings, an alien being might reasonably ask: "How does the human perceive the environment?" and "Where is the memory?" If such a being had the capacity to see that there are nests of cells in our bodies that are permanent while other cells come and go, it would see that these same cells are the basis for the functions of perception and memory—that they are the "essential" cells, the center of the abiding individual and the basis for the persistence of the self in a human being. The alien would reasonably assume that we human beings take special precautions to protect the vitality of our essential cells. Like queen bees, the irreplaceable and endangered essential cells of the immune and central nervous systems must be afforded a special degree of security, nutrition, and respect.

If you now realize that you have irreplaceable nests of cells that help you perceive and remember your experience of the world and that are the basis for the persistence of yourself, you may ask what needs to be done to ensure their vitality. At the very least you would conclude that your essential cells should have the best food and should avoid toxic substances.

Here are seven steps aimed at keeping your permanent cells healthy. The same steps provide a useful checklist for anyone with a chronic health problem or a desire to maintain vitality.

How do I come up with such a list? I keep track over time of the successes and failures of people who've come to me with chronic illnesses. After thirty-five years as a practitioner, certain simple, safe, and inexpensive approaches frequently come up as winners for people with all sorts of problems, so they rank high on the list. Other approaches, even if they are not simple or inexpensive, are on this list thanks to common sense, a reading of the current medical literature, and learning from the experiences of individuals who have had dramatic and convincing results. Such is the case, for example, with mercury toxicity.

1. **Treat dysbiosis.** Dysbiosis refers to an imbalance of the germs that live in your digestive tract. Even a single dose of an antibiotic can produce long-standing disturbances in the balance of this important population of friendly and unfriendly germs in your body. The thing that has surprised me the most in my work as a physician is how frequently exploring this option turns up striking, and sometimes miraculous, responses in people who have suffered from chronic health problems. The range of these problems is enormous and disquieting to physicians who hold to a single cause–single effect view of disease. Removing yeasty foods from your diet, taking measures to reduce the overgrowth of fungus in your intestine, and reducing your intake of refined carbohydrates can be accomplished in a matter of two to three weeks. In a fairly short time, and with relatively little inconvenience, you will know whether this factor has a bearing on your problems.

2. **Avoid food allergens.** Depending on whom you ask, you will get very different answers if you say, "I am reading this book where it says that food allergies are a common cause of chronic health problems. What do you think?" Still, looking into the question of food allergies can be quite simple. First, you have to consider the possibility. Second, you have to try to identify some relationship between what you have eaten and the symptoms that you experience. What is not so simple is the timing of the whole process.

3. **Investigate gluten sensitivity.** Gluten is the sticky protein in wheat, rye, and barley. Sensitivity to it is not the same as an ordinary allergy. Getting someone to do an experimental three-month trial of eliminating gluten from his diet, even when severe symptoms are the target for the remedy, is a tall order. The average person and most doctors simply cannot believe that difficulty with the digestion and biochemical or immunological processing of the gluten found in these grains can cause substantial mischief. This dubiousness is curious in view of one well-recognized illness—celiac disease—that is well known to be the result of intolerance to gluten. Gluten intolerance affects approximately one out of a hundred people; if you look among sick people instead of in the general population, you will find a much higher incidence. If you have problems of just about any combination of symptoms you can name or even if you have been diagnosed with a disease and remain symptomatic, a brief avoidance of gluten in your diet will cover this base.

4. **Eliminate mercury.** Twenty-five years ago, I would only rarely have suggested to a patient that she get mercury-containing fillings removed from her teeth and that she avoid frequent consumption of large fish. Now, I believe that everyone should have mercury amalgam fillings removed. Certainly, if you are troubled by a puzzling chronic health problem, this strategy should be somewhere in the top ten considerations on your list of things to try.

   While continuing to deny that this recognizably toxic substance is a problem when placed in people's mouths, dentists in North America put 7,000 tons of mercury in individuals' teeth every year. Weighing the evidence on both sides of the extremely polarized debate over the safety of mercury sulfur amalgam, I am astonished to find that the American Dental Association still defends its 1930s decision that mercury amalgam fillings are safe. Nowhere else can I think of such a wide gap between a public policy such as this one, proclaimed by the American Dental Association, and the private policy you may wish to enact for the sake of your own health. In the hands of a dentist skilled in the use of the new compounds, amalgam replacement can be relatively quick and painless. For information, see the website of the International Academy of Oral Medicine and Toxicology at www.iaomt.org.

5. **Supplement with folic acid.** What originally tipped me off to the importance of folic acid was the nearly perfect record it has had in reversing the precancerous changes that are indicated by abnormal Pap smears in women. In addition, folic acid supplementation to prevent birth defects in babies has become a matter of public policy.

One might wonder, then, whether there may be in the pipeline an extension of public policy with regard to the other benefits of folic acid supplementation, particularly in the realm of cancer and cardiovascular disease. So far, the published studies suggest that the general use of folic acid supplementation would reduce heart disease, cancer, and a variety of other woes more than any other single change you could make in your diet and environment. Those of us who take a supplement of folic acid and get immediate results are a tiny minority compared to those whose use of folic acid will result in long-term benefits.

6. **Take fatty acid supplements.** The immediate effects of supplementation with omega-3 fatty acids, such as those found in fish oils and flax oil, are so noticeable in many people that arguments for its healthy properties need not be too strong from my side. While the direct benefits are generally skin deep and include changes in hair, skin, and fingernails, understanding the chemistry of fatty acids (as described in Chapter 10) should persuade you that the overall effects of fatty acid supplementation are much more profound.

7. **Consider vitamin and mineral supplements.** Folic acid differs from most of the other vitamins because it does not have a number like B_1, B_2, or B_{12} associated with it. It is, however, a B vitamin by virtue of its having been thrown into that category when vitamins were grouped during their

discovery in the first half of the twentieth century. Other vitamins and nutrients, such as minerals and amino acids, play crucial roles in the body's chemistry for getting rid of unwanted substances. Most nutrients easily can be assigned to some particular function in the body. Detoxification is such a nutritionally demanding but general process that nutrients to support detoxification chemistry are important, but they do not easily boil down to a simple recipe.

2

Toxicity from Without

WHEN I LIVED in Chad as a Peace Corps volunteer in 1968, the capital (now Njemena) was called Fort Lamy. Fort Lamy was more of a capital village than a capital city. Seen from the air, it was a sprawling version of the mud brick houses found in villages scattered thinly across the part of Chad that enters and then occupies the eastern Sahara Desert. Except for periodic forays by truck to "the bush," as the countryside was known, to visit and supervise my covolunteer nurses and technologists in various population centers, I made my way around Fort Lamy on my bicycle, an unheard-of means of transportation for any of the small contingent of foreigners living in Chad as part of the diplomatic, foreign aid, and French military communities. None of the contingent of less than two dozen physicians in all of Chad, most of whom were French military, would be seen driving anything but a Peugeot or a Land Rover. My job was to look after Chadians and to lead our Peace Corps team of nurses and technicians. I was surprised, therefore, to have a messenger arrive at my gate late one evening with an earnest request from a large Asian nation's ambassador to Chad. His seven-year-old daughter, Sue, was acutely ill and I was asked to attend to her. As she had better transportation at her disposal than I did, it was arranged that I see her immediately in my cubicle at the Peace Corps office, which was a short walk from my gate.

Acute is an ambiguous medical term that can mean sudden, recent, and/or serious. The distinction between acute and chronic illness is not completely clear, but it is entirely central to many of the issues I would like to clarify in this book. Many medical practices that apply to acute illness are not appropriate when applied to chronic illness, particularly the belief that naming the problem is equivalent to understanding it. Some medical lessons learned from acute illness are, however, instructive in understanding the mechanisms that may lie beneath chronic illness. The lesson I learned from the ambassador's daughter still keeps me on my toes for any kind of illness I confront in my life as a physician.

The child was prostrate. Her condition was one of deep stupor combined with a high fever. Responsive to painful stimuli, but not apparently hurting in any particular place, she had become suddenly ill on the preceding day. Another physician had advised her family that it must be *un coup de paludisme* (malaria attack) which is the Chadian equivalent of the American pediatric refuge "it must be a virus," except that the advice comes with specific recommendations that various antimalarial measures be augmented. Facing another long night with an increasingly sick child, the ambassador had called my ambassador seeking someone to give a second opinion. Ambassador Morris, a Harvard graduate, reassured him that my worst past indiscretion was having gone to Yale, where I was to return at the end of my Peace Corps stint from Chad to serve as chief resident in pediatrics. After Sue and her parents and I had settled down in a space that bore no resemblance to an examining room, I took a careful history, which turned out to be all too simple. Sue had been in robust health and protected by immunizations and regular malarial prevention medication until the day before. Since its onset, her fever and lethargy had been unremitting—unlike malaria, which usually gives a pattern of fever broken by sweats. She had not complained of pain and her bowel movements and urination, while infrequent, were otherwise unremarkable. She had had no respiratory symptoms and no family member or playmate had been sick. The most important question on my mind was, "What terrible disease *doesn't* she have?" Even if a patient is not worried about having an awful disease when consulting a doctor with a headache, abdominal pain, or occasional numbness in the fingers, a doctor's first job is to rule out the worst possibilities: a brain tumor, an appendix about to rupture, multiple sclerosis. Once the worst possible considerations are off the list, then the more optimistic side of the detective work can begin.

I studied my patient as she was carried in. She was just aware enough of her surroundings to know she did not want to be there and gave me a meeching* look. Her skin was flushed and hot to the touch. Her temperature, taken under her arm, was over 104.7°F (40°C). Meningitis or encephalitis ranked high on the list of worst possibilities, so I started by looking carefully for evidence of these as I examined her optic nerves with my ophthalmoscope, checked for a lack of suppleness of her neck and spine, checked her reflexes and her muscle tone. She was weak but nowhere paralyzed. Encephalitis would have been the trickiest diagnosis to rule out on the basis of a physical exam. I was prepared to do a spinal tap. Otherwise my technical and laboratory resources were limited to what I could do with my own senses, aided by my microscope. It took only a few minutes to complete my physical examination, which revealed absolutely no localized sign of an infection that could explain the girl's condition.

I began to discuss the next possible steps with her parents, and none of the choices were ones they wanted to consider. I explained that I had fervently hoped to find a treatable cause of her problem, such as an ear infection. Since the 1950s, when antibiotics brought quick cures for many infections, finding "something to treat" became almost more satisfying than being able to report to worried parents that it is "nothing serious."

When I was an intern and resident in pediatrics at Yale, the expression "midnight ear" summoned the ambiguities of finding "something to treat." It is midnight in the emergency room. You have been on duty since 7 A.M. and have fourteen hours still ahead, some of them, you hope, asleep in the emergency room on-call bunk. A cranky child with a history of congestion and a fever awaits your decision while his worried and weary parents pray that the young doctor before them knows what he's doing. "I can't find any specific trouble, and I think he will be just fine if you take him home and keep an eye on him overnight" is not

---

*Meeching means a look that pleads "I am helpless, please do me no harm." Dr. Louise Bates Ames taught me this word, explaining that it is a good old New England expression.

nearly as good an answer to their prayers as "He has an ear infection, and an antibiotic should take care of the problem." Even if there is no specific treatment, a specific name is needed. If the doctor can name it, he can tame it, or at least that is a common fantasy. As a worried and weary resident I prayed that careful examination of such a child's eardrums would reveal enough redness to justify the hoped-for denouement. An eardrum that was just red enough for weariness and hope to take it over the threshold to treatability was a "midnight ear." If a small heap of earwax prevented the young doctor from easy visualization of eardrums, the potential for frustration demanded a mature conscience. Should the wiggling child be tormented with attempts to clean the ear, with the attendant risk of scratching the surface of the ear canal? The resulting spot of blood coming from the ear canal, however medically trivial, could be horrifying to a fear-struck parent inferring that the young doctor, who seemed OK until a moment ago, had just perforated the child's brain. Such situations gave rise to a pediatric rule of doubtful accuracy, that a red eardrum is never found behind a wall of wax.

I had honed my skills at nontraumatic wax removal and I summoned my confidence in those skills as I began to discuss the situation with Sue's parents. They had watched me take extra time examining her right ear with my otoscope. Could the problem be there, they asked, hopefully. "I think not," I said, because I had seen enough of her eardrum to be pretty sure that an ear infection could not explain her serious illness. Most ear infections in a child her age would not produce an illness like hers anyway.

As I spoke, I was still bothered by the dark brown smooth appearance of her earwax. Asians tend to have flaky or dry earwax, and when I was trying to see Sue's eardrum around the obstruction, I theorized to myself that her fever had melted the wax into the brown bead that obstructed my view. I am not sure why I stopped theorizing out loud to the ambassador and his wife to reexamine Sue's ear. I guess I realized that I had never seen such smooth wax in any child's ear, no matter what degree of fever had been present, and the melted wax theory just wouldn't fly. I could imagine no relevance of the abnormal wax but was reluctant to dismiss any unexplained detail.

I explained that there was still a chance that some redness of Sue's right eardrum lurked behind a dome of wax that had kept me from being able to see the whole drum, but in the urgency of the situation I really just wanted to buy a little time to collect my meager thoughts. I carefully inserted my otoscope and inspected the wax until it transformed itself into the body of an engorged tick. Sue had a tick in her ear! Now I had to deal with further uncertainty. I was already in doubt as to which of several options would be the safest course for Sue. Now I had to contend with the risk of getting sidetracked by the delay and potential trauma involved in attempting to dislodge a critter known for its tenacity and whose presence was likely to be completely irrelevant to Sue's condition. I imagined the consequences of spending precious time trying to get the tick out when I should have been doing a spinal tap or sending Sue to the hospital to be cared for. The ambassador and his wife were especially resistant to the latter option, because they knew that the needles used there were sometimes not properly sterilized.

I put some mineral oil in Sue's ear canal in an attempt to start the process of suffocating the tick while I pondered what to do. A spinal tap would have been much easier than trying to manage the tick with my head mirror and a pair of tweezers. I decided to go for the tick, as I realized that there was at least a possibility that the tick was making Sue sick. Madame Ambassador held the lamp from which the light reflected from my head mirror into Sue's ear canal; the ambassador held Sue tightly and I prayed for a steady hand.

I had just completed six months of a residency in obstetrics and gynecology before coming to Chad. Perhaps the skills I had learned there would see me through this delivery. I lined up the beam of light with Sue's ear canal, drew a bead on the tick, and then obscured my view as I inserted the forceps that I hoped would embrace the tick. No big game hunter in the wilds of Chad could have felt the thrill I experienced as I withdrew my instrument with the quarry intact. While Sue's parents and I shared the first moments of this small triumph, we all realized that now we must get back to the main business at hand. Scarcely had we retrieved our pre-tick seating arrangement when Sue stretched and sighed deeply. Within three minutes she roused from her stupor, left her father's lap, and embraced her mother. Within fifteen minutes her body temperature dropped. Within a half an hour we three astonished and relieved grown-ups ushered the smiling and chattering

Sue to the ambassador's Mercedes-Benz. She was back to her normal self. I was not. I was forever changed.

I walked back through my gate in the warm midnight air with the shrill sound of Fort Lamy's insects squeaking, chirping, and singing in my ear, feeling the elation of a do-gooder who has done some good and pondering a serious scientific question: "What was that?" An extraordinary reaction to an ordinary tick bite? An ordinary reaction to a tick bite in an extraordinary location? Would you call the substance injected by the tick an allergen or a toxin? It was a variation on the theme of tick paralysis caused by several kinds of ticks around the world, particularly in Australia where they take a significant toll on sheep, who succumb to their paralytic bite. Sue had tick toxicosis, and the form her illness took probably had to do with the location of the bite. The substance in the tick saliva may be viewed as venom or as an allergen, since it evidently affects different individuals differently.

Sue's illness and the quick recovery impressed upon me a lesson I cannot ignore when considering the possibilities in any patient's illness: do not overlook the chance that a person may be having a peculiar reaction to something. Frequent findings of such "somethings" bring me back to the phrase my pathology professor, Avril Lebow, repeated like a mantra: "Illness results from the interaction between an etiologic (i.e., causative) agent and a susceptible host." Some people have peculiar interactions with etiologic agents that we would not expect to make a person sick. These experiences have changed me from a doctor who focuses on finding, naming, and treating diseases to one who focuses on finding and treating the unique interaction between my patient as an individual and toxins and allergens. *Individual* is the key word. Each of us is different. There are more differences among individual humans than there are differences among other creatures of a given species.

Sue did not have a disease, even though there is a name for her condition. She had a quirky response to something the tick introduced into the skin deep in her ear canal. A disease is a concept we form about a group of ailing people who share common features. Acute illness usually fits into characteristic patterns so that we easily form a concept of the group features that encompass, say, chicken pox, or a cold, or an attack of kidney stones. In such cases human individuality becomes submerged beneath the more or less uniform effects that some germ or trauma evokes. As a physician I am expected either to name the problem or to eliminate several likely (and worrisome) prospects. It is like going to the woodshed with my flashlight to investigate an unexpected noise. I should return saying "It was a raccoon" or "I could smell a skunk" and assume that I had eliminated the possibility of a prowler. Many acute illnesses fit their statistical images. They are as identifiable as a raccoon or a skunk glimpsed or sniffed in the woodshed. Most acute illnesses can be learned the same way a naturalist learns to identify robins and wrens or maples and oaks by a few identifying features. Sue's illness was not like this. It was very much the unique response of a particular little girl to a particular kind of tick injecting a particular something into a particular place in her ear canal. Another little girl, another kind of tick, or another location of the tick would probably not have produced the illness that I saw.

Sue did not have a germ. For example, Lyme disease is transmitted by ticks who deliver a particular germ with their bite. The tick must be attached for several hours before it can inject the *Borelia bergdorfi* germ. After that the germ must multiply so that it may be hours before a noticeable redness appears on the skin and days or weeks before other manifestations of illness occur. I get tick bites from time to time working outdoors in our part of Connecticut, which is heavily populated with ticks. The bite may itch for days after removing a deer tick or dog tick from my skin, so I know that even when no *Borelia bergdorfi* germs have gotten into me, there was something in the tick's saliva that caused a little reaction. Sometimes, in me, as in many people, the skin returns to normal as soon as the tick has been removed. So if the "something" that the tick injected into Sue was not a germ, which would have remained after the tick was removed, and if it was like the substance that often gives me an itchy spot, how could she have reacted in such an extreme way? Whether you call Sue's reaction toxic or allergic, it planted a question in my mind that I now ask about each patient I see, even when I know the name of his or her illness: "Could some part of this person's illness be due to a toxin or an allergen?" The question that naturally follows would have been unanswerable in Sue's case but is worth pursuing in individuals with chronic illness: "If there is a toxic or allergic component, why is this person unable to rid herself of the toxin or why is she sensitive to the allergen?"

Before moving ahead, let us review some of the main points that I have raised, which will be discussed further as we proceed. First of all, we need an approach to illness that goes beyond naming the illness and suppressing the symptoms with drugs or other approaches that fail to identify the cause. Secondly, the cause is not always simple, but can result from a complex interaction of different kinds of imbalances within an individual. The notion of balance includes *getting* the right amount of substances to satisfy our individual needs and *avoiding* exposure to substances that are toxic or allergenic. Achieving such a balance is relevant to the protection of a group of cells within one's body that are permanent and undividing and thus make up the essential cellular self. The cells in question reside in the immune and central nervous systems and, as such, participate in an individual's capacity to perceive and remember. Protection of these cells involves optimizing the function of the transient cells of the body, which, among other functions, rid us of potentially harmful substances.

3

The Map

USING THE MAP on page 27 as a tool for understanding health problems is not much different from the kind of thinking you would do if the Swedish ivy plant on your windowsill failed to thrive. The following two questions would precede any attempt on your part to make a diagnosis, in the sense of giving a name to the ivy's condition beyond "not doing well," "wilting," or "withering." You would first consider whether you failed to give the plant something it requires to flourish and then wonder if the plant might have been exposed to something that did not agree with it. If you know anything at all about horticulture, you would understand that these two questions are interconnected. If a plant is stressed by pests, germs, or toxins, it may require more nutrients; if it is undernourished, it may be more susceptible to the effects of pests, germs, or toxins. Human beings are more complex than Swedish ivies in that we need a greater variety of nutrients and are subject to a greater variety of germs and toxins, but the most important difference between us and ivies is that there is a greater variety among us than there is among Swedish ivies.

The pioneer nutritional biochemist Roger Williams[1] pointed to a 200-fold difference in calcium requirements among different healthy human subjects. Recent research in the toxicity of mercury has revealed sensitivities to mercury that vary as much as a millionfold from one individual to another.[2,3] During a period early in the twentieth century when babies were given mercury-containing teething powders, the mercury poisoning known as pink disease that ensued had a greater than thousandfold difference dosage threshold from one infant to another. That is to say that it took more than a thousand times less mercury to make one child sick as compared with another.

Why is it that we are all so unique? I am privileged to have as a friend Charles Remington, Ph.D., emeritus professor of biology at Yale, one of the world's foremost scholars in the field of insects and evolutionary biology. During butterfly watching and pleasant evenings in front of the fire sharing his vast knowledge of biology, he has explained to me that individuals in a species tend to vary more if their habitat has been disturbed. For example, if you study all the creatures in a certain area and observe variations in color, size, and other characteristics of individual members of a given species of bird, insect, or mammal, they will resemble one another closely if they have all been living in the same undisturbed habitat for many generations. Then, if there is a major disruption caused by fire, flood, deforestation, or other calamity, the species who remain to repopulate the territory will go through an extended period in which they will show marked diversity among individuals until the environment achieves a new stability.

Treating the Individual—*Not* a Diagnostic Category

We human beings are quite consciously aware that each of us is different from everyone else. I don't think that the notion of our individual uniqueness is a conceit. It is firmly based on biology and probably is enhanced by the fact that our habitat has changed as much as that of any creature during the last few thousand years of migration, the establishment of agriculture and the addition of thousands of new chemicals to the human environment. However, it is easier to group people to avoid the complexity of thinking about and treating each person as an individual. Supposing I were to fill out an insurance form for a patient and report that he has John Doe's disease and that I am giving him the John Doe treatment. The map that I will show you in this chapter makes the purpose of thinking about individuals much clearer, but it does not help with insurance forms. It has been forty years since Roger Williams's research and writing introduced a new paradigm for medicine backed by solid scientific research. It is not a lack of science that has retarded the blossoming of a medical practice focused more on individuality. It has more to do with the inertia of a medical hierarchy that yields slowly to change and the strong investment of various levels of the hierarchy in treating diseases, not individuals.

It is not just that doctors think in terms of diseases but that a whole structure of fund-raising, allocation of resources for research, reimbursement for medical care, medical education, and specialization is based on the idea that diseases exist in nature as fixed entities. We do not need to give up the idea of diseases nor yield to the understanding that our picture of disease is a transient artifact of our limited ways of seeing groups of individuals. We can begin to improve on our system for taking care of individuals, with or without having a name for their disorder, by applying a simple strategy for problem solving. I invite you to consider such a way of thinking about any chronic complaint that you may develop, whether your chronic symptoms fall neatly into a diagnostic category or whether they cannot be summed up under a given disease name.

The Individual Approach

If we take the strategy for treating Swedish ivy and apply it to any chronically ill person, a logical question flows from each of the first two questions.

1. What kinds of things does this person need to get in order to thrive?
2. What kinds of things does this person need to avoid in order to thrive?

By current knowledge, the kinds of things a person needs in order to thrive are vitamins, minerals, fatty acids, amino acids, accessory nutritional factors, light, healthy rhythms,* and the ability to love and

---

*See Baker, S. M. *The Circadian Prescription*. New York: Putnam Perigee, 2000.

be loved. When I first began thinking along the lines of the map, I was intimidated by my lack of knowledge of nutritional biochemistry and the environmental factors associated with allergy and toxicity. It seemed to me that the disease-oriented approach, which I had mastered to a certain extent, was a more comfortable domain in which to think about problems. Soon, however, I realized that there is an elegant simplicity to the map that is governed by the realities of biochemistry and of our environment: there are only so many nutrients and accessory nutritional factors and there are only so many foods, inhalants, and toxins to which a person can be exposed.

By current knowledge, the kinds of things a person needs to avoid in order to thrive are allergens, which are things that, in small amounts, bother some people more than others, and toxins, which also vary in their capacity to bother a given person but are more uniformly harmful. Just about any substance can act as an allergen. Therefore it is helpful to break the possibilities into categories to make the prospects less overwhelming. Those categories are food, pollen, dust, animal dander, chemicals, mold, and other microorganisms. To be considered as a possible cause of problems a substance has to be in either one of the two ways each of us divides the universe: our insides or our outsides. That may seem like an unnecessarily naïve point, but it speaks to the question of whether the strategy is thorough. It is reassuring to think that one's view of possibilities is all-encompassing and that nothing is overlooked before one begins to whittle them down through a process of elimination.

When it comes to toxins, the possibilities are: elementary substances such as lead, mercury, and aluminum; compounds produced by living creatures including ourselves and our germs; and synthetic compounds, most of which are products of petrochemicals which in turn come from seriously decayed oil that was once produced by living creatures. Radiation of various kinds is potentially toxic as well.

The Map and How It Is Used

Following is the map with an emphasis on the point that this strategy is not a substitute for the standard medical approach that includes taking a history, doing a complete physical exam, and conducting laboratory tests to make a diagnosis with special attention to thinking of all the worst things that could be wrong. The map serves as a guide whether my patient has a *definitive* diagnosis such as diabetes, Crohn's disease, or psoriasis; a *descriptive* diagnosis such as hyperactivity, depression, or tinnitus; or a collection of symptoms that match no diagnostic category. It may be relatively easy to accept that if symptoms match no diagnostic category, then the map may serve as a guide to finding out what is wrong. It may be difficult to understand how the map can be helpful for people who already have a diagnosis. Having a diagnosis implies that the condition is more or less understood. That is just the problem. Having a label for a problem may lead to the conclusion that all symptoms are "caused by" the diagnosis. Further thinking tends to stop more easily than if the basic question of what is wrong is left unlabeled and open. Remember that the most common mistakes that we doctors make are the result of finding one thing wrong and being lulled into a relaxed frame of mind about further detective work. I call this being "blinded by the obvious."

Map for a Thorough Approach to Health Problems

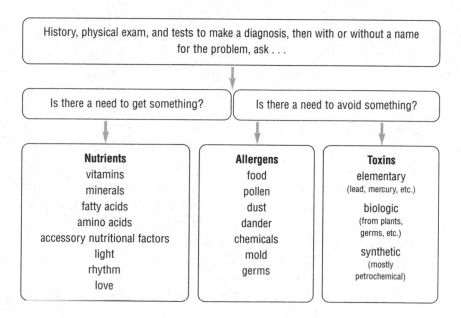

History, physical exam, and tests to make a diagnosis, then with or without a name for the problem, ask . . .

Is there a need to get something?   Is there a need to avoid something?

Nutrients	Allergens	Toxins
vitamins	food	elementary (lead, mercury, etc.)
minerals	pollen	
fatty acids	dust	biologic (from plants, germs, etc.)
amino acids	dander	
accessory nutritional factors	chemicals	synthetic (mostly petrochemical)
light	mold	
rhythm	germs	
love		

In explaining this map to patients I recruit their participation in the diagnostic process. Even after patients have filled out a twenty-page questionnaire and written a chronology of their major life events, illnesses, operations, schooling, jobs, losses, and successes, additional clues emerge when reviewing this strategy. For example, a woman recovering from surgery and chemotherapy for her metastatic breast cancer once consulted me wondering what she might do to maximize her chances of staying well. Her history seemed quite lacking in risk factors, and her initial biochemical and immunologic evaluation was surprisingly free of the kinds of abnormalities I would have expected. In reviewing the situation with her I repeated my recitation of the map, covering each item in the diagram as I described its logic. When I mentioned toxins she asked if there could be any significance to the fact that her home had a strange odor. The house was built of natural cedar, and a preservative, pentachlorophenol, was then applied to all the interior and exterior surfaces. The odor was quite like cedar and was at its strongest in certain interior spaces, particularly a nook where their dog, now dead of cancer, had slept. I referred her to my associate, Dr. Bob McLellan, a specialist in occupational health. Her tests revealed a level of pentachlorophenol in her urine that was substantially above the maximum permitted in workers in a pentachlorophenol factory. During the ensuing months her home was treated to seal in the toxin so that it could neither be touched nor inhaled, and she and her husband were given supplements to support their detoxification chemistry. She remains well today and is content to be uncertain whether her long-term exposure to a chemical toxin had a role in her susceptibility to cancer. Doubts about the connection never made it seem reasonable to leave the situation alone. Her husband died of leukemia last year.

The map is not a menu for doing lab tests. Most of the factors listed can be evaluated with lab tests, but the map is simply a guide to a complete list of questions beginning with the word *could*. "Could this person have a magnesium deficiency or a special need for magnesium that contributes to his or her problem? Could this person have accumulated an unhealthy amount of aluminum that is contributing to his or her problem?" The literature on the incidence of deficiencies or special nutritional needs and the prevalence of toxins in our environment provides ample scientific backing to the legitimacy of at least posing the question. It is beyond the scope of this book to explore all of the laboratory tests that cover each consideration in the map. The next chapter will describe tests that constitute the highest priorities with respect to evaluating the chemistry of detoxification.

How People Become Sensitive

The part of the map that refers to allergies carries another implied question that arises when sensitivity is a factor to be considered. The question is, "If this person is sensitive to one or more substances that contribute to his or her illness, then how did he or she become sensitive?" Why are people sensitive anyway? We know what sensitivity is: it is a reaction to something that does not bother most people at all or at least not to the same extent. It can be called allergy, hypersensitivity, or intolerance without much precision in distinguishing among those terms. We know how to recognize it and I will share with you some ideas I have about how people become sensitive, but we really do not know precisely what changes when a person goes from having a normal tolerance for a food, pollen, animal dander, chemical, mold, or germ to having an intolerance. Certain lab tests are helpful, but even if I were able to peer anywhere into a person's cellular makeup, down to the level of molecules and up to the level of organization of a person's electromagnetic fields, I would not know where to look for the thing that has changed from the time before he or she became sensitive to milk, eggs, strawberries, mold, or perfume. We know that the capacity to become sensitized is a capacity shared by the nervous system and the immune system, which provides further evidence for their unity. We know the kinds of cells that are involved in sensitivity in each case, but we do not understand the changes in those cells that account for their change in "attitude." Without knowing exactly where sensitivity is, it is still possible to find reasons why people become sensitive.

I began accumulating the following list from listening to the stories of patients who came to see me with problems of sensitivity to many things, sometimes so many things that controlling their diet and environment seemed a fairly unworkable treatment compared to finding the sensitivity's basis and repairing that. The list provides a helpful orientation to considering ways to evaluate a person's detoxification chemistry, which I will cover in Chapter 9.

1. **Something is out of balance.** If I am standing on one foot and you push me over with your thumb, I could conclude that I am thumb-sensitive and need to stay away from thumbs. Now if I put both feet on the ground, I regain my balance and I am no longer so sensitive to the effect of your thumb. In the same way, a toddler with eczema may itch all over and keep himself up half the night scratching because of sensitivities to foods, fabrics, dust, or other factors that cannot easily be determined. He seems sensitive to just everything. Then, for example, if a zinc or fatty acid deficiency is found and his balance is restored with respect to zinc, his sensitivity will diminish.

2. **Something is wrong with digestion.** If the destructive forces of digestion are lacking and more than normal quantities of food substances escape being stripped of the antigenicity by which they are able to provoke allergic reactions, then it is the fault of digestion, not the immune system. I realize that I am being unfaithful to the whole integrative medicine concept by starting to cast blame on this or that system. However, once allergy is provoked by poor digestion, digestion may be the victim of allergy. So it goes round and round in a circle. Circular effects are the rule.

   Magnesium deficiency provides another example. A person under stress tends to lose excess magnesium as part of the response to stress. A magnesium deficit then creates the setting for less resistance to stress. The question is not so much which part of the circle is to blame, but which is the most practical place to intervene to break the cycle. If a person is sensitive to most foods and has very poor stomach acid secretion or a failure to produce good bile or other digestive juices, then supporting those functions with supplements makes more sense than severe dietary restriction.

3. **Infection.** If the immune system has to get up every day and fight germs, it is not surprising that it may become cranky and overly reactive to environmental stimuli. I think that "hypervigilant" is a good term for describing the posture of the immune system that has taken on an increased reactivity to many kinds of substances. Such a posture is part of a state of immune activation that is common in individuals with many illnesses including autoimmune conditions, chronic fatigue immunodeficiency syndrome, and childhood autism as well as generalized tendencies toward allergy. The place in the body where germs are least accessible to control by our various immune mechanisms is the intestinal tract, where parasites and the overgrowth of yeasts are the most common provokers of a hypervigilant immune system.

   If I meet someone casually and he or she describes a relative's problem and says no more than that the person in question was quite well until a certain point when he or she became suddenly sensitive to all sorts of foods, chemicals, or dust, my very first thought is that the person must have been on antibiotics in the interval before the onset of the state of hypersensitivity which was caused by a yeast problem. Virus infections are also capable of a tenacious chronicity, and the ones that have the greatest capacity for ongoing subtle mischief are herpes simplex and Epstein-Barr virus.

4. **Chemical exposure.** An exposure to any potential allergen can sensitize a person if the exposure is intense or if it is accompanied by a high level of stress, even if the stress is not painful. When I joined the Peace Corps I had finished my six-month stint as an assistant resident in obstetrics and gynecology and suddenly found myself getting up early in California not to deliver babies but to play soccer with Peace Corps volunteers who were just out of college and in much better shape than I. Leaving my cat, car, house, and belongings to be cared for by someone else for two years and traveling with my then wife and nine-month-old daughter across the country constituted stress. When I started having to get

up at night to treat myself for asthma attacks, I suspected that I was having some sort of emotional reaction to the Peace Corps. A vacationing friend of my wife's then returned to claim her cat who had been boarding with us, and my asthma disappeared. My severe cat allergy lingered and some years later I realized that my sensitization must have had something to do with the cat-stress combination, especially considering that I had had cats all along. Returning from Africa after two years I found myself unable to tolerate my old cat's presence!

If, instead of being exposed to a cat, I had moved into an environment that was contaminated with formaldehyde, pesticides, or petrochemicals, I might have not only overloaded my detoxification system's capacity to rid myself of my daily load of inhaled or ingested material, but something more insidious could have happened: the engendering of a global state of sensitivity to *all* chemicals. Such a state stretches scientific credulity. First of all there has been a long-standing belief in the field of allergy that only fairly large molecules can provoke an allergic response and most of the substances we informally group under the heading "chemicals" are small molecules. Moreover, they are a diverse group, and allergy is understood to be quite specific. Finally, the symptoms reported by victims of chemical sensitization are often cerebral and subjective in nature, inviting the reproach that "it is all in your head." Individuals who suffer from chemical sensitivity often find themselves in a surprisingly adversarial medical setting in which physicians state firmly that they "do not believe in" chemical sensitivity and cite the finding of emotional disorders in chemically sensitive patients[4] as evidence that there is no physiologic basis for the problem, which therefore must be a state of malingering or psychosis. A person who has become chemically sensitized enters a much more polarized medical setting than someone who has been sensitized to cats, and should be forewarned of encounters with physicians who hold strong positions that whatever is wrong with such patients is "not real."

The controversy over chemical sensitization, sometimes referred to as multiple chemical sensitivity or MCS, has been explored thoroughly in Canada, where the Ministries of Health are obliged to take definite positions regarding the eligibility of patients for benefits and physicians for reimbursement in connection with MCS. The report of the Environmental Hypersensitivities Workshop of the Ministry of Health in Ottawa states in its executive summary:

> Given its clinical prominence and the attendant socioeconomic costs, multiple chemical sensitivities (MCS) is worthy of scientific study. In the meantime, however, the patient should not be caught in the medical debate and denied social benefits. Benefits should be based on defined functional disabilities, not on the medical label. Ministries of Health should be responsible for ensuring that there is no discrimination against patients by insurance companies in regard to coverage for medical-related expenses.

The MCS controversy has been investigated by the State of New Jersey, which commissioned a study by Nicholas Ashford, Ph.D., J.D., and Claudia Miller, M.D.[5] Ashford and Miller provide detailed support for the concept of chemical sensitivity. The United States Department of Housing and Urban Development has adopted a clear, legally supported policy recognizing chemical sensitivity as a disability requiring reasonable accommodations by landlords.[6] The Social Security Administration recognizes MCS as a disabling condition in the sense that a person may have the physical capacity to perform work, but if unavoidable environmental exposures cause debilitating symptoms, a disability exists.[7]

The concept of sensitizing potential was first championed by the late Dr. Theron Randolph, who became the father of an ecologic approach to medicine and teacher of many of us who found ourselves in the practice of various specialties, knowing a great deal about our patient's innards and very little about their "outards," that is, the physical and chemical environment with which their chemistry interacted.

Although Dr. Randolph's work coincided in the 1960s with the general awakening to the realities of chemical pollution as a widespread phenomenon, the medical profession's focus on disease left it poorly prepared to accept the very individual nature of chemical sensitivity and slow to accept the idea that a patient's toxic burden might constitute a clinical priority no matter what his or her disease may be.

Dr. William Rea is the Randolph disciple who has done more than anyone to bring a passionate and scholarly energy to the study and treatment of problems of chemical sensitization and chemical poisoning. His multivolume treatise, *Chemical Sensitivity*,[8] presents the most comprehensive review of the subject. Dr. Sherry Rogers's books[9] provide another rich resource of information about chemical sensitivity.

5. **Adrenal insufficiency.** Here is a story that exemplifies a common finding in sensitive individuals. Abigail Stockwell was at the Sleigh House restaurant one evening in 1980 when an obstructed flue filled the place with gas fumes. She was among dozens of patrons who were treated in the emergency room for a variety of symptoms from fainting, nausea, and headache to numbness and tingling. One of the puzzling things about chemical exposures is the great variety of symptoms that can be produced in different individuals from an essentially identical exposure. Before that exposure she was well except for a childhood history of eczema. After it she was troubled by fatigue, nausea, a peculiar scratching pain in her head, difficulty concentrating, and depression. Such symptoms would recur particularly following exposure to a variety of petroleum-based products. Pumping her own gasoline could make her sick for a couple of days. She was bothered by certain foods as well as by pollen, dust, and molds. When I first interviewed her I thought that she was sensitized by her initial exposure to gas fumes and that her recovery

would be more difficult to achieve than it would be for someone with sensitivities limited to foods or mold. I asked her about symptoms of fatigue, feeling cold, recurring infection, low blood pressure, poor modulation of blood sugar, salt craving, acne, and other hormonal symptoms such as excessive facial or body hair or loss of scalp hair. These are all indicators of a common condition (about one in 100 people) called congenital adrenal hyperplasia (CAH). The only symptoms she reported from the list were hair loss, fatigue, and feeling cold in the evening. I did not think that she was a very good candidate for CAH. After failed attempts to treat her by removing mold from her diet and killing yeasts in her intestines, I did a simple test to rule out CAH which involved a trial of treatment while monitoring her symptoms with a key lab test before and after the trial. Here is the information I gave her and the instructions for the brief test treatment.

Low-dose hydrocortisone therapy

Hydrocortisone is the normal product of your adrenal gland. It is the main hormone among a whole family called steroid hormones. Some people fail to produce enough hydrocortisone to provide for their body's needs. Like people with low thyroid function, such people benefit from taking hormone pills to make up for what their body fails to produce each day. The average daily production of hydrocortisone in your body is about 30 to 40 mg. If you have adrenal insufficiency (low adrenal function), you may be producing only 15 to 25 mg daily and consequently may feel cold and tired and have many sensitivities, low blood pressure, and salt craving. By supplementing your low production with, say, 5 to 20 mg of hydrocortisone, your body's supply becomes normal and symptoms should promptly disappear.

The big misunderstanding that occurs with regard to this treatment comes from the use of high-dose cortisone or cortisone-like medicines (prednisone, Medrol, etc.). With high-dose treatment, doses way in excess of your body's needs are given and have a serious drug effect plus many side effects: high blood pressure, weight gain (usually with a characteristic central distribution and a moon face), immune suppression with a tendency toward fungus infections, diabetes, stomach ulcers, and so on. These potential side effects have nothing to do with what could happen with low-dose hydrocortisone treatment, which cannot give your body significantly more than your body needs. Even if your production of hydrocortisone is already normal, the extra 5 to 20 mg hardly ever makes a noticeable difference. High-dose treatment employs amounts of cortisone or cortisone-like drugs (such as prednisone) equivalent to at least several times your body's daily output, that is, 60 to 300 mg of hydrocortisone per day.

So, if a friend says, "Oh my God, you're not taking cortisone, are you? That stuff is so dangerous, my mother took it and it gave her ulcers and she gained weight!" please reassure yourself and your friend that you are using this medicine in a totally different and safe way. Can tests be done before actually taking this treatment to determine if it is really needed before trying it? Yes, but the tests are very good at picking up people with bad adrenal insufficiency, but they can miss people who need low-dose hydrocortisone treatment. I have done the tests in dozens of people and have decided that the best first test is a clinical trial of hydrocortisone. It is without risk and takes less time and trouble than the tests. If you fail to feel better from taking the hydrocortisone, then you don't need the test. If you feel much better, so that it appears that you needed the hydrocortisone, then a test can be done later to confirm the diagnosis, if that seems appropriate. Note that low-dose hydrocortisone is used to treat people with mild adrenal insufficiency in whom the symptoms of underproduction of hydrocortisone come out as an overproduction of the "male" type of hormones that in women lead to scalp hair loss, excessive hair growth, and other hormonal abnormalities.[10]

Dosage schedule

Start with 2.5 mg (a quarter of a 10-mg tablet or half of a 5-mg tablet). Take a dose of 2.5 mg daily between 6:00 and 8:00 A.M. over the course of a week. See how you feel. If nothing has happened, increase the dose to 5 mg between 6:00 and 8:00 A.M. and observe any changes in symptoms for another week. If at any point you develop carbohydrate cravings, experience bloating or insomnia, feel hyper, or have any other negative symptoms, either stop or reduce the dose. If at any point your target symptoms (fatigue, excess hair growth, sensitivities to allergens or chemicals, acne, salt cravings, or feeling cold) begin to improve, discuss with your doctor a strategy for finding the lowest dose that will produce the best effect. You may increase your dose and change the timing of your intake to 10 mg in the early morning, 5 mg at noon, and 5 mg at

4:00 P.M. before concluding that your experiment has failed. At that point you will be taking about half your body's need for hydrocortisone to supplement what you presume your adrenal glands were not producing. If the experiment is a success, you have the following obligations:

1. To establish, by trial and error, the optimum dose. This can be done only by finding the lowest dose that will keep symptoms under the best control.

2. To explain to doctors that the basis for treatment with low-dose hydrocortisone is a successful clinical trial, the results of which were very convincing. You should anticipate that most doctors will reject this way of making the diagnosis. If it turns out that you will continue to need the low-dose hydrocortisone treatment for more than about six months, then it would be reasonable for you to undertake the kinds of urine and blood tests that are normally used to document adrenal insufficiency. It is still my position that the diagnostic trial you have just undergone is more decisive than the laboratory tests; there are individuals who have convincing response to treatment but who would not qualify for treatment based on the lab tests.

3. To be aware that what you are taking is hydrocortisone, *not* prednisone. Many people, including some doctors, are unaware that the potency of the two is very different. For example, 5 mg of hydrocortisone is the same as about 1 mg of prednisone.

4. If you are in an accident or undergo severe physical stress, such as surgery, your doctor should consider doubling the daily dose of hydrocortisone. This is not because the dose you are taking suppresses adrenal function (as high-dose prednisone would do) but because your diagnosis of mild adrenal insufficiency indicates that you are probably not able to mount a normal adrenal response to stress.

Mrs. Stockwell became 50 percent better after the first few weeks of treatment when she had arrived at a dose of 2.5 mg of hydrocortisone four times daily. After that she went on to make a complete recovery and now can go about her business in New York City with only occasional symptoms when she encounters the exhaust of a diesel bus or someone wearing too much perfume in an elevator. As part of her initial evaluation I had done a study of her detoxification chemistry. After she was treated with the hydrocortisone, it became completely normal. The normalization of her detoxification chemistry provides a good example of the interconnections among immune function, adrenal function, and detoxification. It may turn out that after a few months of treatment she will no longer need her hydrocortisone.

Adrenal insufficiency can result from a congenital weakness in the biochemistry that forms hydrocortisone in the adrenal gland. In its extreme form it produces a masculinization of girl babies to the point that their clitoris and other external genitals are enlarged to a male appearance. Unless the condition is recognized immediately the associated imbalance in the regulation of body salts can precipitate a fatal crisis. At the very least, a delay in the proper assignment of gender can result in distress for everyone involved. Many people with adrenal insufficiency have a very mild form of the same condition. They do not have genital abnormalities but may show, after maturity, salt cravings, excess hair growth, and acne as well as the other symptoms mentioned above. On the other hand, an unknown percentage of individuals with adrenal weakness acquire it from stress. This was first studied by Hans Selye, the famous physiologist whose studies of soldiers killed in battle clarified the relationship between the adrenal gland and stress. A certain number of the healthy seventeen- to twenty-year-old young men who are found dead on a battlefield have no wounds to explain their death. At postmortem examination, the only abnormality found is an exceptional shrinkage of the adrenal glands. These and other studies conducted by Dr. Selye over many years gave rise to the whole modern concept of the relationship between stress and health. In a sense, my profession received the concept of stress with open arms but not so with the findings about the adrenal glands. The reasons for that turn of events are discussed in the monograph[11] by the endocrinologist William Jefferies. Considering Mrs. Stockwell's lack of long-term masculinizing symptoms and the sudden onset of her illness after a chemical exposure, I think that her condition may be temporary so that in several months or a year she can come off the hormone support and find that her health and tests are normal.

6. **Invasive life events.** In the course of a two-hour initial visit, patients with multiple sensitivities often refer to the unforgettable pain and anger of experiences suffered in childhood that were abusive, often in a very literally invasive way. This abuse need not always have been sexual, as described in Chapter 1; even certain medical procedures (such as a tonsillectomy performed in the kitchen, believe it or not) could easily be interpreted by a child as a violation accompanied by severe pain. For some the revelation of such stories had gone unspoken for many years. Especially in respect to sexual abuse, if feelings of anger and pain do not find their natural exit in speech they are more likely to burrow into a person's soul and do mischief that may be expressed more immunologically than psychologically on the surface. When such patients have pursued the appropriate psychological treatment, the immunologic aspects of their hypervigilance become much more responsive to treatment.

This may be the appropriate place to make the point that I do not think that health is concerned only with biochemistry and immunology. I have chosen those subjects for this book to clarify the central role of detoxification chemistry, but I do not mean to suggest that words and deeds and the feelings they engender cannot be toxic. On the contrary, I believe that words and deeds have the greatest potential for both harm and healing and that only when they are in the right balance can the biochemical and immunological treatments prevail. We live, however, in a culture with a high level of psychological awareness. If a person is feeling chronically sad without apparent reason, appropriate attempts to find a psychological reason or to alleviate symptoms temporarily with drugs should not fail to include a look for biochemical balance.

4

Toxins from the Gut

I HAVE A special interest in airplane crashes because my father died in an airplane crash when I was thirteen and my mother's only brother died in another plane crash when I was twelve. My dad's crash was the first major plane accident in which there was a successful legal effort to prove that human error had been the cause. Years later a small settlement was shared by families and lawyers that pressed the case. When I recently heard in the news of an American Airlines jet that crashed on its approach to Cali, Colombia, I was intrigued that within days of the crash, pilot error was cited as the cause. Then came the news that alcohol had turned up in the intestinal contents of the pilot. The final story was that the pilot had indeed made navigational errors, but the alcohol was present as a result of "natural processes" that occur after death. He had not been drinking. The alcohol was not a by-product of the pilot's metabolism. Nor is alcohol a part of any molecule that could release it after death. Thus, it could be mistaken for the residue of a gin and tonic consumed during life. But where did the alcohol come from?

Fermentation

Sugar is the common source of energy for all living things. When it burns clean and releases all of its energy, the carbon, oxygen, and hydrogen atoms in the sugar become water and carbon dioxide. When we burn the sugar (glucose) that appears in our blood after we eat, the "smoke" that comes from that burning is made of water and carbon dioxide as is the smoke from a candle flame, a cigarette lighter, or a municipal incinerator. The municipal incinerator may burn dirty, yielding a lot of soot and ash; however, when the body burns glucose, it is clean and simply produces pure water, pure carbon dioxide, and energy. Even though glucose does not burn dirty, it can burn incompletely so that the sugar molecule is not broken down to its most fundamental components but rather, into pieces that carry two or three of the six units (carbon atoms) of which the sugar was made. The two-unit product is alcohol and the three-unit product is lactic acid, which is familiar as the sour taste in yogurt or sauerkraut. Germs can make alcohol and lactic acid. Humans can make lactic acid, but not alcohol. The intestinal contents of the body of the airline pilot contained alcohol because the germs normally present in the intestine went on to continue producing alcohol as they had done in life. The alcohol accumulated because the pilot's liver was not available to detoxify the alcohol as it was produced. He, like everyone, was making about half an ounce of alcohol in his intestines every day. He, like everyone, was taking this alcohol into his system until death extinguished his metabolic fire, but not that of the germs that lived in his gut.

In life, the burning of the alcohol results in its detoxification. It goes up in smoke. One of the reasons it is toxic, however, is that it *must* be burned. Unlike other foods, including the lactic acid found in foods, the body cannot treat alcohol as something to be stored and saved for later. Another reason that alcohol is toxic is that it interferes with the chemistry of living things.

Alcohol exercises its toxic effects in a variety of ways. The pickling effect of high concentrations of alcohol used as antiseptics or preservatives gives an erroneous image of the way alcohol may affect a living cell in the concentrations found where germs have released it. In such concentrations as well as in concentrations found in the blood and tissues of someone drinking alcoholic beverages, alcohol interferes with many different enzymes. Enzymes are large molecules that embrace smaller ones so that the latter can be assembled or disassembled. Alcohol has a particularly bad effect on a group of enzymes called cytochrome P450 that are the main workers in the body's detoxification system. In this way alcohol can function as a sort of master toxin, enhancing the toxicity of all other toxic substances and even turning a relatively harmless substance such as the common pain reliever acetaminophen (such as Tylenol) into a poison by seriously interfering with a person's ability to detoxify the acetaminophen. Alcohol also interferes with the activity of key enzymes in the transformation of fatty acids into hormones as discussed in Chapter 10.

Next time you go past the liquor store, replace in your mind's eye the sign that says "Peter's Spirit Shop" with one that says "Fungal Toxins Sold by the Bottle." Everything in the store was made by fungi. Wine, beer, whisky, vodka, sake, tequila, and rum are all made by fermenting the sugars found naturally in grapes, grains, cactus, or sugar cane. The kind of fungus used by vintners and brewers and distillers occurs naturally on the surface of the fruits of every plant. Various species of the fungus are found in soil, in the air we breathe, and living on the moist surfaces of our body. The fungus stops short of completely burning its supply of sugar and forms alcohol, which it tolerates more than some of the other germs that might compete with it for space in nature. The fungus's self-protective knack for producing alcohol was domesticated by our ancestors between ten and twelve thousand years ago when someone discovered that grape juice would develop special properties when left in a jar with the lid on. Later on, someone discovered that wheat flour could be leavened with some of the residue from the wine-making process, and that subsequently the residue from the leavening could be passed on in the dough, some of which could be saved as a "starter" to make more dough. The particular fungus in question constitutes a large fungal family called *yeasts*. The ones we use for brewing and baking started out as the same ones found in nature on the surface of grapes. Eighteenth-century Dutch experimenters found strains of yeast that were more suitable for brewing and others that were more suitable for baking, and Louis Pasteur completed separation of yeasts that we now distinguish as baker's and brewer's yeasts. In baking, the alcohol produced in the leavening goes up the chimney during the baking process. With wine-making, it is the carbon dioxide that leaves the brew and escapes into the air, so that, with the exception of beer, champagne, and other sparkling wines, the alcohol is retained within the beverage while the bubbles of carbon dioxide escape.

When the Body Becomes a Brewery

It was champagne that brought down Angela Carino. Wedding champagne. After two glasses she began calling the mother of the groom a slut and threatened to kill the young man serving shrimp on a silver tray. After another half glass of bubbly fungal toxin extract she fell on her face into a yew shrub. Her son and three other men carried her 200-pound limp body from the scene and it took sixteen hours for her to recover her senses and two weeks to heal the lacerations she suffered from the fall. Her reputation is still scarred. At one time, Angela had had a normal tolerance for alcoholic beverages. Then she had a stomach bypass operation after failing to lose much of her 300 pounds by less invasive methods including dieting. After the bypass procedure, she became an alcoholic. Her special relationship with alcohol is simple from one perspective: she shouldn't drink. However, she does drink, and the consequences are devastating. From another perspective, it is complex: she can manage moderate amounts of expensive champagne or a fresh wine made by her European brother-in-law. Her response to drinking a couple of glasses of Dom Perignon is pretty normal. However, if she drinks champagne priced at less than $10 a bottle, she turns violent at first and then sinks into a kind of stuporous, toxic impairment of brain functioning. Many of us experience a milder reaction that varies with the quality of the champagne, reminding us that it is not the alcohol but other components of the wine that can contribute to its delayed disagreeable effects. I like champagne, but if it is inexpensive it gives me a terrible headache, so I just say no.

After ten years that have nearly destroyed her life, Mrs. Carino is in the process of learning that her operation turned her into an alcoholic. The operation did not change the amount she drank. It did not change her usually sweet and generous personality. It allowed her to keep her weight closer to 200 pounds and it did something to her intestines that drastically altered her response to alcohol. How so? She became more sensitive. She became sensitive to something more likely to be found in inexpensive champagne than in expensive champagne or some other wines. It has to do with alcohol, but it is not only the alcohol. It is the *congeners* or substances other than alcohol that are produced in the process of aging and fermentation.

The ambassador's daughter was unusually sensitive to a tick bite in a way that had to do with the type of tick and the location of the bite. Angela Carino's sensitivity is different. She went from having a tolerance for wine that was more or less like other people's to becoming peculiarly sensitive to it after her intestines were rerouted to send food past the point where it could be easily absorbed and turned into fat. Instead her food now gets used by a host of germs that inhabit a part of her intestine that would have previously been only thinly populated with germs. What do her germs do with the food? They eat it, or, more properly stated, they ferment it. After her operation, Angela developed a sort of brewery in her own intestines. The yield of her internal brewery is not only triggered by cheap champagne. It is produced by a mélange of unpredictable, more or less toxic products of fermentation that include alcohol. Her detoxification chemistry now has to cope with a daily load of toxins that it never had to deal with before, and it can no longer handle the extra load of alcohol and its congeners. I will return to Angela Carino's story later.

Charles Swartz went to doctors complaining of neurological symptoms: inability to concentrate and episodes of inappropriate behavior. The diagnosis was elusive until a blood alcohol level was checked and found to be elevated. Normal levels are nearly zero, but some people have trace amounts of alcohol in their blood produced by intestinal yeasts. His levels were similar to those produced by drinking alcoholic beverages, but he emphatically denied consuming any alcoholic beverage and he, like many alcoholics, was thought to be a liar. Further investigation showed that he was absorbing alcohol produced by yeasts in his own intestinal tract. These yeasts were rewarding their host for his hospitality by consuming sugars from his diet and converting them to alcohol. His case was widely reported[1] and became a source of inspiration to lawyers defending drunken drivers. Mr. Swartz's circumstances were unusual, however. He, like Mrs. Carino, had had intestinal surgery and he had lived in Japan, which was the presumed origin of the mutant yeast with a special capacity for intestinal alcohol production.

Antibiotics and Yeast Overgrowth

Charles Swartz and Angela Carino each had had intestinal surgery, providing an altered habitat for the germs, which in Mr. Swartz consisted of some Japanese brewing mutants and in Mrs. Carino consisted of other factors that produced alcohol and other toxins that altered her response to drinking. A more common way to alter the germs of the intestinal tract is to kill large numbers with antibiotics.

Earl Knight consulted me with peripheral neuropathy after he had read Dr. William Crook's book, *The Yeast Connection*.[2] Earl was in perfect health when he consulted a physician at age eighteen for his college physical. The examining doctor noted the pimples on Earl's back and face and suggested that he take tetracycline, the antibiotic most often used for treating acne. Earl took the antibiotic for three years pretty regularly, and the pimples diminished. When Earl stopped the treatment his acne flared and became a mass of cystic lesions on his face, back, and chest that were still a major problem when he came to see me nineteen years later. In the intervening years, and beginning at the time of the tetracycline treatment, Earl first developed a diffuse eczema with red, itchy, sometimes cracking and crusting skin eruptions on his entire body with intense localization on the backs of his knees and the crooks of his elbows. When the cracks became infected, the dermatologist gave him antibiotics. Earl also struggled with depression and fatigue. After reading books by Adelle Davis, he tried vitamin and mineral supplements, which actually made most of his symptoms worse.

Vitamin and mineral supplements may not make you feel better, but they really should not make things worse. The dangers of nutritional supplements are limited to rare instances of unwise excess or imbalance in the way they are taken. For the most part the body knows how to handle these substances, which, unlike drugs, are a familiar part of one's biochemistry and are not toxic in a wide range of dosages. Why is it that some people report a variety of unpleasant symptoms when they take supplements? Earl, for example, experimented with all sorts of exceptionally pure supplements and repeatedly found that some of the B vitamins intensified the disabling burning of his hands and feet for which he consulted me in 1988. His reactions to vitamins, even those that might normally be prescribed for treating peripheral nerve problems, were so severe that I was reluctant to experiment with injecting vitamins to see if a different route of administration would make a difference.

I put Earl on a yeast-free, mold-free diet and prescribed medication to kill the yeasts in his intestines. After Earl's problem was under control, and his vitamin intolerance was still present, my assistant, Jayne Barese, suggested that we try injections of B vitamins. No adverse reactions occurred and the shots gave Earl a boost of energy. Earl's prior difficulty with vitamins illustrates a common problem signified by intolerance to vitamins. In nearly every case it turns out to be related to the mediation of germs inhabiting the upper intestinal tract. The germs get hold of one or another vitamin or mineral for which they have a particular affinity and celebrate by producing extra amounts of whatever toxins it pleases them to produce. The toxins, liberated in the intestines, either provoke digestive complaints or they are absorbed systemically where they provoke all sorts of symptoms, depending on the person. In Earl they provoked the precise symptoms of which he complained during several years of misery before Dr. Crook's book led him to me. His hands and feet were on fire most of the time. He had a sensation of numbness that was more like wearing heavy gloves than an absolute extinction of his sense of light touch, pressure, pain, or finger position. He is a professional violinist, so wearing his neuropathic gloves was a special burden.

When Earl first consulted me he had already experimented with his diet along the lines outlined in Dr. Crook's book. He avoided fermented and leavened foods and other fare that is or becomes yeasty. Orange juice, like other juices one buys at the store, for example, picks up some of the yeasts that naturally inhabit the fruit's surface. During the preparation of the fresh juice or concentrates used in making commercial juices, the few yeasts that get into the juice to begin with multiply so that they become quite abundant in the finished product without causing noticeable fermentation. There is nothing wrong with having a few yeasts in our juice any more than there is a problem with inhaling the many yeasts and parts of yeasts and other molds that are present in the fresh air we normally breathe. Earl found, however, that his symptoms improved significantly when he avoided bread, vinegar, commercial juices, unpeeled fruits, and leftover food. His fatigue, depression, rash, cystic acne, and peripheral nerve symptoms got worse when he broke the diet.

It is rare for a person to actually harbor a strain of baker's or brewer's yeast in his or her digestive tract. Usually any yeast that is consumed live on fruit or dead in bread disappears during the process of digestion. Earl Knight's sensitivity to yeast in food was caused by the overgrowth of other kinds of yeasts that flourished in his intestines when other normal germs were killed by the tetracycline he took for acne. These yeasts probably existed in his digestive tract in normal quantities before he took tetracycline. With the antibiotic, they became so numerous they may have crossed the line from being normal intestinal germs to causing infection. The other species of yeasts that had become bothersome when consumed in food were not infectious, but they produced a toxic allergic reaction in Earl. When I encouraged him to continue his yeast- and mold-free diet and gave him medication to kill the yeasts in his intestine, nearly all of his problems cleared up except for a remaining intermittent sensation of tingling in his fingers and toes that may have been an acceptable disability in a nonviolinist. Subsequent removal of his dental amalgam and several courses of dimercaptosuccinic acid (DMSA) to reduce his body burden of mercury cured his remaining symptoms.

A New Look at the Yeast Connection

Before I met Dr. Orian Truss in 1977, I knew that yeast was a relatively innocent germ with a capacity for causing stubborn vaginal infection, often provoked by taking antibiotics. The prevailing medical opinion then, as now, was that yeast infections were associated only with superficial problems, most of which could be seen through a vaginal speculum. Yeast germs were thought to become truly infectious only in people whose immune systems had been injured by cancer chemotherapy or radiation or in babies who might get a thrush infection in the mouth even if they had not been given antibiotics. It is common knowledge that people can have strange reactions to germs, such as the allergic reaction to strep germs that results in rheumatic fever. I had not considered that the yeast germs that normally inhabit the intestines could constitute an allergen, however. I knew that people could have allergic reactions to foods, but I did not think of yeast and mold in food as high on the list of possible offenders as are egg, wheat, milk, soy, chocolate, and seafood.

On the other hand, I had already begun to reassess my diverse experiences with yeasts. Before going to Africa in 1966 I had done part of a residency program in obstetrics and gynecology. In Africa I trained midwives and treated many gynecologic problems. Most of the women I saw had never taken any antibiotics. Yeast infections were rare in those women. In the United States, however, from the introduction of sulfa drugs in the 1930s and antibiotics in the 1940s, the incidence of vaginal yeast infections had risen to epidemic proportions, until today there are TV advertisements for antifungal treatments to be undertaken based on self-diagnosis. I also appreciated that one woman might harbor what seemed to be a very small number of yeasts when seen through a microscope in a drop of vaginal secretion and yet she would have tissues that appeared to be scalded by the infection. Another woman might have mucus that was loaded with the kind of actively branching yeast that are supposed to be the hallmark of active infection and yet she would be completely free of symptoms at the time of a routine examination for a Pap smear. Dr. Truss's findings helped me reexamine what I had been taught. I began to think about what I saw in my patients in a new way.

Dr. Truss had seen a number of patients in his allergy practice who experienced a dramatic remission of illness when he treated what had seemed to be unrelated symptoms of respiratory allergy with desensitization and avoidance of yeasts and molds. Following a trail that was indicated by his early patients, he accumulated a body of evidence over a ten-year period leading to the publication of his first papers and, in 1982, his book, *The Missing Diagnosis*.[3] One has only to try out his simple concept on a few patients, such as Earl Knight, to see how easy it is to spot and treat individuals who have been sick for years.

By the time I saw Earl I had been including Dr. Truss's concepts in my thinking about chronic illness for more than ten years, during which time Dr. Truss and I had organized two international conferences on the subject. We had hoped to establish a dialogue between practitioners who, using the most benign kinds of intervention (a yeast-free diet and a trial of antifungal medication), could easily see results in their patients, and academicians, whose reverence for the established truth creates a skepticism that is invaluable to one's professional thinking.

There has always been a dialogue in my profession between empiricists and rationalists.[4] Empiricists are those of us who believe what we see and rationalists are those who see what we believe. It seems to me that the belief system of modern medicine has become something of a handicap in permitting us to see well. If this were not the case, Dr. Truss's theories would have gained widespread acceptance long ago. Instead, many members of the medical profession stubbornly refer to the truth as that which is revealed in medical texts and editorials produced by committees and they fail to simply verify the yeast problem's validity with a few patients, as I had done after meeting with Dr. Truss.

The two conferences we organized were intended to bring together a faculty of clinicians and academicians and an audience of clinicians anxious for guidance on how to help patients, many of whom had diagnosed their own problems as yeast-related with the help of Dr. Truss's book. The first conference, held in 1982 in Birmingham, Alabama, was a success, particularly because it brought about a respectful dialogue between clinicians who had direct experience with patients who had convincing histories and responses to yeast-free diets and antifungal therapy, and academicians whose experience tended to be more focused on hospitalized patients with yeast problems. The second conference, held in San Francisco in 1985, was well attended but was disappointing because two of our main speakers canceled at the last minute. They were pressured to stay away by the organized opposition of a major medical society, which denounced the yeast idea as heresy, partly because of rivalry with an organization that cosponsored our conference and provided continuing education credits for attending physicians. Leaders in infectious disease and immunology have since retreated from their strong denunciation of the ideas put forward by Dr. Truss, but some of the public statements and editorials of the 1980s are still quoted by various authorities to threaten the livelihood of physicians who treat patients with yeast problems and to deny insurance reimbursement for such treatment on the grounds that it is not medically sound. In fact, there are groups of doctors in various states who fancy themselves quackbusters and go after the licenses of colleagues who treat patients with yeast-free diets and antifungal medications.

Much of the credit for bucking the tide of orthodox medical opinion regarding yeast goes to the late Dr. William Crook, whose wit and sincerity have disarmed many skeptics to the point of at least acknowledging that there might be such a thing as a yeast problem. He organized the very first yeast conference in Dallas in 1980, attended by a couple of dozen of Dr. Truss's first converts. Soon Dr. Crook was turning out books, which have sold widely and spread the word among many people who would otherwise never have gotten help.

In 1995 William Shaw, Ph.D., published a report[5] on finding fungal organic acids in the urine of children with severe developmental problems. Dr. Shaw's observations have given us an important method for documenting the presence of yeasts and other abnormally abundant intestinal germs and have supported a new understanding of the mechanisms by which they work their mischief.

The smoke from any fire is acid. (The ashes are alkaline.) The smoke from the metabolic fire of a living being bears more complex molecules than does the smoke from a hot fire where things are more completely broken down. Each of us produces from our metabolism small amounts of organic acids as part of the smoke from our metabolic fire. Organic acids can be measured in urine much as they check the exhaust of your automobile to see if the engine is well tuned. A serious blockage in chemistry can produce excessive amounts of a particular organic acid, so doctors check for such abnormalities as a way of diagnosing metabolic diseases in children. Milder disturbances in the pattern of organic acid excretion can reflect subtle imbalances in chemistry that are similar to the problems of a poorly tuned engine and can also be remedied by adjustments in a person's intake of nutrients. Prior to Dr. Shaw's discovery, laboratory scientists measuring urinary organic acids dismissed the finding of certain organic acids in the urine of patients based on the knowledge that these organic acids were not produced by the metabolism of the patient but were the product of the collective metabolism of all the germs, or flora, of the patient's intestines. Each of these gut germs has its own tiny metabolism and many of them have evolved ways of competing with one another by producing toxic substances. Alcohol production by yeasts is just one example of a variety of chemicals produced by bowel germs that find their way from the bowel into the bloodstream where they pass through the kidneys and into the urine where they can be measured side by side with organic acids of human origin. Dr. Shaw said, in effect, "Organic acids produced by the fungi (yeasts) of the human intestine may poison us by interfering with our chemistry." He presented the cases of children who had seizures and severe developmental problems that resolved with the elimination from their intestines of the germs that produced the organic acids that Dr. Shaw had found in their urine. His findings have led to the use of organic acid evaluation as a diagnostic tool in children and adults with abnormalities of intestinal flora, including the overgrowth of yeasts and certain bacteria. Quantitative tests for organic acids can be obtained from the following laboratories:

MetaMetrix Laboratory, 800-221-4640 or 770-446-5483

Great Plains Laboratory, 913-341-8949
(holds the patent for the use of urine microbial organic
acids in autism)

Great Smokies Diagnostic Laboratory, 800-522-4762

Dietary Fiber and Hormone Regulation

What do the germs of your intestine like to eat? They will eat just about anything, but dietary fiber feeds good intestinal germs, which discourage unfavorable ones. I can think of few other topics in medicine that have flip-flopped as has fiber. In my training I was taught that fiber was a useless, inert ingredient in our foods and we should all look forward to the day when, like the astronauts, we could subsist on some sort of highly refined goop that provided us with just the right ingredients for physiologic prosperity. Out of Africa came Dr. Dennis Burkitt, who, while practicing medicine in Uganda, noticed that Africans eating a traditional diet had a completely different pattern of illness than those people, including those of African descent, eating a Western diet. The dietary content of roughage, fiber, or indigestible cellulose that makes up the main structural component of plants is what accounted for the fact that Africans were spared most of the diseases that affect us, from diabetes and heart disease to appendicitis and hemorrhoids. My own African experience gave me firsthand exposure to Dr. Burkitt's ideas.

Of the many ways that fiber promotes good health, such as providing bulk and holding water plus the many positive influences on dozens of problems from acne to ulcers,[6] there is one you probably have not heard about. This one should open your mind to the integrative medicine factors linking diet, the germs that live in your intestine, antibiotics, hormone balance, and cancers of the reproductive organs such as breast and prostate. From time to time we hear that a particular substance has been declared safe or unsafe based on whether or not it causes cancer or at least leads to mutations in the DNA of living things, a marker for a cancer-causing potential. As you can appreciate from the examples I have given, there are many ways that an unwanted substance can bother a person that have nothing to do with cancer, and in some ways the preoccupation with cancer tends to put people off track. Even when preoccupied with cancer causation, I think we hear too much about environmental toxins as compared to ways we can enhance our repair mechanisms, such as those involving folic acid, which enable us to keep our DNA fresh and undamaged. As you read on, I hope you will keep in mind that cancer may be a more easily grasped and feared consequence of the chain of events being described than, say, hormone imbalance. When visiting a doctor, a patient is much more likely to hear that the hormones are a little out of balance than that he or she has cancer, yet this is usually by way of saying that there is not any real problem and that the imbalance "just happens" and is not really subject to remedy. After all, it is not a disease.

Imbalance, however, is the precursor of disease. Imbalance may be associated with symptoms that a person or his or her physician may deem insignificant because they do not constitute a disease. However, imbalance worsens all illness as it progresses, even when—in the case of trauma or infection—the illness may begin in a person who is in a state of balance. A person with "insignificant" symptoms of hormonal imbalance may take a special interest in the evidence linking long-term subtle effects of certain kinds of dietary fiber with the ultimate effect of prostate and breast cancers.

For many years epidemiologists have recognized that the incidence of reproductive cancers (breast in women and prostate in men) is much higher in populations consuming a Western diet as compared to the vegetable-based diet consumed in most of Asia, Africa, and South America. The incidence of bowel cancer, cardiovascular disease, and other problems varies in the same way.

Dr. Herman Adlercreutz (professor of clinical chemistry at the University of Helsinki) developed a theory that something in fiber mediates the healthy effects of a vegetable-based diet. He was particularly intrigued by statistics that showed a low cancer incidence in Finns and others consuming a traditional rye bread that is made from the whole grain and leavened not with yeast but with a culture of *lactobacillus* (acidophilus)—the same kind of germ that ferments yogurt and sauerkraut. It appeared that consumption of rye bread was associated with an exceptionally low reproductive cancer incidence for Finns as compared with other Europeans who consume wheat bread. Dr. Adlercreutz's theories were not accepted by the scientific community when he first proposed them, as fiber was thought to be unnecessary or at least inert. It is understood that reproductive cancers are stimulated, after their inception, by higher levels of hormones (estrogen in women and testosterone in men) so that if, apart from any hormonal influence, such cancers appear, then factors that contribute to high hormone levels would favor the persistence and growth of such cancers. For his theories to be true there would have to be a substance present in, say, rye fiber, that would do one of the following:

1. Inhibit high levels of sex hormones during the life of the individual so that in the event of a cancer arising, it would not be stimulated.
2. Limit the actual growth of cancer cells themselves.
3. Hinder the development of blood vessels that a cancer requires around itself for nourishment.

Cancer-Inhibiting Foods and How They Work

Dr. Adlercreutz and others have amassed convincing data showing that compounds called isoflavonoids and lignans isolated from rye fiber and soy protein and various other vegetable sources will modulate sex hormones and inhibit cancer growth and the nourishment of cancers by surrounding blood vessels. The use of isolated compounds in research does not imply that their use as isolated substances will be forthcoming. There is a strong argument for the use of certain nutritional supplements as isolated compounds, e.g., folic acid. In the case of the fiber-derived compounds, Dr. Adlercreutz points out that "it should be kept in mind that it is to be preferred to consume original food, or food modified only slightly, instead of consuming isolated or synthetic compounds."[7]

When someone eats a piece of whole rye bread, most of the protein, carbohydrate, and fat is digested in the stomach and small intestine so that the available molecules of amino acids, sugars, and fats pass into the bloodstream, leaving behind a residue of material that is carbohydrate in nature but resists digestive efforts to separate the sugar molecules of which it is composed. It originally comes from plant cells where it forms their walls. These walls are stiff and sturdy as opposed to the flexible and delicate membranes of animal cells. Cellulose is mashed but kept intact for the making of paper. Cellulose molecules can be dissolved and manipulated to produce celluloid and rayon, but they can only be digested into their component sugar molecules by bacteria. Such bacteria in the intestines of my two goats are the only means they have of digesting their hay and leaves, but we humans lack any such bacteria in our gut. We do not have bacteria that liberate the component sugars from cellulose so that we can burn the sugar for energy. Our bacteria do, however, liberate substances from dietary fiber. We can then absorb these compounds into our bodies. Certain bacteria of our intestinal flora are the only way we have of extracting from fiber the compounds that perform the three cancer-inhibiting functions noted above. Dr. Adlercreutz's research has shown the absence of such compounds from the bowel and blood of individuals who have taken antibiotics. The compounds stay absent for a prolonged time, more than three months, so that if these people were to take an antibiotic, twice a year, they might inhibit the production of the cancer-preventing compounds half of the time. The protective compounds from soy do not need the mediating effects of bacteria, but can be absorbed during digestion of the soy protein. Numerous experiments demonstrate correlations between levels of the substances from rye fiber and soy protein (as well as from flaxseed, sesame seed, various grains, and tea) and the growth and incidence of prostate and breast cancers in animals and in humans. The collective research in this area has been published in dozens of articles since the 1970s. Another decade may pass before specific recommendations emerge from the scientists who are most intimately involved in this research. Yet another decade may lapse before we hear official recommendations for dietary change or supplementation. In the meantime those of us who are familiar with the research may find it prudent to consume whole rye bread leavened with *lactobacillus* and to increase our intake of soy protein, tofu, or miso soup. Obviously, those allergic to rye or soy must avoid these foods.

Toxic Hormones

The relationship between dietary fiber, hormone balance, and risk factors for reproductive cancers (breast in women and prostate in men) is covered extensively in my book *The Circadian Prescription*.

Hormone balance changes with age, season, exposure to toxins, hormone-containing foods, and emotions triggered by love and loss.

The efficiency of your detoxification chemistry has an impact that you can understand when you realize that your supply of any given hormone is influenced not only by how much of it you make every day but by how efficiently you rid yourself of used hormones. The same chemistry that deals with other leftovers from your body's metabolism as well as unwanted toxins from the outside world is devoted to neutralizing hormones and ushering them from your body when you are done with them.

A Boy with Breasts

Newborn boys and girls have breast buds resulting from estrogen hormones that have crossed the placenta from their mother. In boys the tissue disappears completely in the first few months of life. Occasionally a girl keeps a little through infancy and childhood until normal adolescent changes lead to normal breast development. Teenage boys may also develop breast buds when they are in the midst of the rest of their adolescent sexual development. They can be a source of embarrassment as well as fear and confusion even if the situation is carefully explained. Boys and girls each have a share of each other's typical hormones, and a slight excess of estrogen or an increased sensitivity of breast tissue to normal amounts of estrogen in a boy may lead to temporary breast enlargement.

I wondered about that connection forty years ago when I was a resident in pediatrics. While seeing patients in the outpatient clinic, I was consulted by the father of a six-year-old boy with breast buds. I figured that if a newborn boy or an adolescent boy could normally have breast buds, then, maybe it could be a normal variant in a six-year-old boy. That boy, Sean O'Malley, had breast buds that made him look as if he were beginning to develop breasts and had caused understandable alarm in his family. My own lack of experience with anything like this symptom in a boy his age led me to jump to the conclusion that he had an estrogen-secreting adrenal tumor.

I admitted him to the pediatric service, ordered the necessary scans, and got a loud scolding the next morning during rounds when the endocrine specialists came around to see him and he was already down in the x-ray department getting his scan. "Don't you know that there have been only eleven estrogen-secreting adrenal tumors in boys reported in all of the world's medical literature?" I had not known that. I took some comfort that my mistake had not caused anyone real harm, but the ridicule I endured before the other residents, nurses, interns, and medical students was painful. The endocrinologists wanted him back on the pediatric floor immediately and recommended blood and urine levels of various hormones before any further steps were taken. A call to the x-ray department brought the radiologist to the phone. "This boy has an adrenal tumor, so we need to take a couple more films before sending him up to the pediatric floor." The scans were completed, the surgeons were called, the situation was reviewed with Sean and his family, and the next morning Sean went to the operating room, where an estrogen-secreting adrenal cancer was removed. His breast buds disappeared within a few weeks and he remained well. The endocrinologists wrote him up and published the case report. I have learned more from my mistakes than from my achievements. Sean provided an opportunity for a little of both kinds of learning.

Luke's Story

Recently I was confronted with the same problem in an eight-year-old boy named Luke. When confronted by Luke's problem, I did not have the feeling that the story would turn out the same way as Sean's; his breast tissue was much less advanced. I was obliged, however, to eliminate the worst possibilities from his list and ordered the necessary hormone levels and scans. They were normal. The puzzle remained. Luke had already been under my care for other problems when the breast buds appeared. As it happened, just before his mother reported his worrisome symptom, I had done a test of his liver's capacity to detoxify various unwanted substances in his body. Had I not done so, I would not have guessed that his endocrine problem might be caused by a problem in detoxifying estrogen. Plenty of boys have problems with detoxification, but I had not seen another case in which it resulted in breast bud development. On the other hand, such a connection is not unheard of. Men with liver disease, such as alcoholics, often develop breast tissue because they cannot rid themselves of the small amounts of estrogen that their bodies produce. Breast development in men with liver damage is, in fact, so common that I figured Luke's symptom could fit that model, given that I knew that his chemistry was somewhat quirky to begin with. I will return to wrap up Luke's story after the following point about detoxification.

Detoxification is what your body's chemistry does to rid itself of unwanted chemicals, whether the chemicals are left over from your own metabolism or enter your system from the air you breathe, the food and water you consume, substances you rub onto your skin or use to treat your hair, or the toxins and allergens produced by the germs that inhabit your intestine. The word *detoxification* is also used to describe a treatment intended to improve or assist this process. Toxins are substances that are more or less harmful in small amounts to everyone. Allergens are substances which, in small amounts, cause harm to one person and not another. Sue's reaction to the tick bite illustrates that the distinction between toxin and allergen is not always entirely clear.

The biologic process of detoxification mostly involves synthesis as opposed to degradation. That is, if you want to get rid of a molecule such as estrogen, your chemistry usually sticks another molecule onto it, making it bigger, but less toxic. Packaged in this way, the unwanted molecule is discharged from the body directly from the liver into the bile where it travels to the intestine and out, or the liver puts the package into the bloodstream where it travels out of the body in the urine via the kidneys. Some toxins, such as heavy metals, find their way out through hair and nails. A minor exit for toxins is through perspiration. For the most part, however, toxins are bundled for excretion from the body by a process that results in a bigger, not smaller, package. I surmised that Luke might be having trouble with the phase of detoxification that deals with the packaging or conjugation of his estrogen.

I had done two kinds of tests on Luke's detoxification chemistry. Several months before, Luke's mother had sent his urine specimen to Dr. Rosemary Warring at the University of Birmingham in England. Dr. Warring is a pioneer in sorting out the connection between childhood autism and a weakness of one of the body's main detoxification systems. This system helps us get rid of leftover hormones, neurotransmitters, and a wide variety of other toxic molecules. Some such molecules come from our own metabolism, like leftover hormones and neurotransmitters, and some come into us with our food or are made by the germs that live in our intestines. This detoxification system—phenosulfotransferases, or PST—seemed normal in Luke, but subsequently I measured other parts of his detoxification chemistry and found that they were seriously under par. I detected the detoxification problems at about the same time that the tests for adrenal tumors and serious hormone disorders were complete, including a careful physical exam in which I assessed his body hair (less than normal for an eight-year-old boy) and the size of his penis and testicles, which were notably small.

When I recommended a treatment with various supplements intended to help the conjugation phase of his detoxification chemistry, I thought that a possible connection between his breast buds and underdeveloped genitals and his detoxification problem was quite speculative and after the scans and hormone tests proved normal, I was prepared to treat the problem with the reassurance that nothing really serious, such as a tumor, appeared to be the cause. I suggested supplements as a detoxification treatment simply because I wanted to do everything I could to improve this crucial part of his overall biochemistry. It was a matter of finding as many things wrong as could be found and fixing as many as could be fixed.

Within six weeks of beginning the treatment for his detoxification problem, he grew hair on his legs, his breast buds disappeared, and his genital size became completely normal for an eight-year-old boy. Of all the various explanations—coincidence, placebo effect, improved detoxification of estrogens—for what brought about this sudden change, I believe it was detoxification that solved the problem.

Luke's story, however unique in my experience, provides a vehicle for understanding connections between toxins, detoxification, and hormones that we hear more and more about but may otherwise have trouble understanding. There are, for example, some pesticides that mimic estrogen. In addition, meat contains estrogens that have been used to fatten animals. The eight-year-old sister of a patient developed breasts, as do an increasing number of young girls these days. I suggested to her mother that she switch to organically grown meat. Her breasts returned to normal. Exactly how each individual responds to exposure to pesticides and estrogens in our food supply must vary as each of us varies. For some of us, our detoxification chemistry is very likely to make all the difference between benign and deadly effects of hormones.

Treating a Toxic Bowel

Many things I learned in school have since dissolved in a flood of evidence from experience and science. My first memory of a conflict between my training and my experience in the real world was in 1968 in Chad, Africa, where I had gone as a Peace Corps volunteer straight from a mini-residency in obstetrics. In Chad I met experienced French doctors who valued supplements of acidophilus, which my American training taught me were unproven and therefore without value. My confidence in my training and my self-confidence (or arrogance) closed my mind to the claims of my French colleagues. Experience eventually changed my mind.

Nowadays, flora replacement, in forms that range from regular yogurt consumption to supplements of various beneficial germs, is widely accepted and has, so to speak, been proven. "Proven" is not as easy as it sounds. Math and physics stand on the relatively firm ground of conceptual and physical laws. Single observations can serve as proof. Medical proof depends on the shaky ground that people are reasonably similar, so that a statistically significant margin of benefit found in a group taking a real treatment proves its advantage over a placebo. Fair enough! But it still leaves any given individual in doubt as to whether the treatment proven for a group will benefit him as an individual. I emphasize this point here because I consistently hear patients express their puzzlement that generous supplements of good flora (probiotics) have neither cured them nor shown up in stool cultures, which continue to show a lack of lactobacillus and bifidobacteria.

When I first started paying attention to the bacterial flora of stool cultures that I sent for parasitology and yeast studies, I thought that restoring the missing good bacteria would be simply a matter of supplying a large enough oral dose for some of the germs to survive the passage through stomach acid and the alkalinity and length of the relatively germ-free small intestine to reach the colon. Sometimes it *is* easy, but often it is not. The following prescriptive suggestions come from my experience with individuals in whom it has not been easy. I suspect that there are in the population many people who can take antibiotics and manage to restore normal flora within a few weeks or months no matter what they do. I think there are others for whom dysbiosis (abnormal bowel germ population) is disabling only in ways that are subtle and long-term, affecting hormone balance and cancer risk. Another group reaches medical attention, where, depending on the interest of the doctor, the dysbiosis may be detected. From that group come the patients who have a very hard time restoring the ecology of their gut.

Ecology is a good word to keep in mind as you think through the remedies. Ecology refers to the interaction of a community of living things in any given habitat. The interactions among the 500 or so different kinds of germs living in your gut are poorly understood but, in principle, dysbiosis is similar to the ecology of, say, a tropical forest where a huge flood, volcanic ash, fire, or removal of all the trees constitutes a trauma from which spontaneous recovery may be very slow or impossible. Simply transplanting all the missing plants and creatures back to the damaged habitat may not work. So it is with taking probiotics.

Naturopathic physicians have a much longer experience than most M.D.s with "reflorestation" of the gut bacteria. I asked Dan Luckaser, a leading naturopathic practitioner and researcher, if I was missing the boat in my efforts to correct dysbiosis in some challenging patients. He agreed that the following steps must be long and strong before some individuals achieve success. Remember that this approach is based on experience with difficult cases, so you have the flexibility to start with the steps that are easiest and least expensive for you. I am no fanatic and I believe that the treatment should be tailored to your needs.

Providing the Milieu

Comparable to providing healthy soil for a garden, providing the material that supports the right environment for beneficial germs is a good idea anyway, but it may be essential for many people who consistently show a lack of good germs in their stool cultures despite taking probiotics. The key is low carbohydrate and high fiber. This means:

1. A fiber supplement of about one tablespoon daily in one of the following forms:
   - Flaxseed ground in a coffee mill to make a fluffy light brown powder (It can be obtained at a health food store.)
   - Psyllium seed powder, also available at a health food store
   - Food-grade cellulose, which can be obtained as Cellulose Powder from Allergy Research Group and available on the Web at www.emersonecologics.com; Phone: 603-656-9778 or toll free at 800-654-4432; Fax: 603-656-9797 or toll free at 800-718-7238; International: 01-603-656-9778; Fax: 01-603-656-9797. Also available from Vital Nutrients by calling 888-328-9992.
2. A variety of these preferred foods:
   - Leafy vegetables (cabbage, lettuce, seaweed) in unlimited amounts
   - Stems and flowers and squash vegetables (broccoli, cauliflower, brussels sprouts, asparagus, squash) in unlimited amounts
   - True roots (beets, carrots, rutabagas, turnips) in somewhat limited amounts (However, these are better than tubers because they are more fibrous, less starchy, and more nutritious.)
   - Beans (green beans; lima beans; soy products; lentils; navy, pinto, black, red, and yellow beans) in unlimited amounts
   - Grains (bread, pasta, rice, corn [maize], millet, rye, barley, wheat, and varieties of wheat such as kamut and spelt) in limited amounts because they are starchy
   - Tubers (potato, sweet potato, yam) in limited amounts because they are starchy
   - Fruits in limited amounts because they are sweet
3. Sugar is a serious no-no because it tends to feed the bad flora and because it is not good for you for many other reasons.

4. Fish, meat, and oils are more neutral when it comes to this question than the other items on the list, so your consumption can be based on taste and other considerations.

Timing is an issue when it comes to taking in carbohydrate. This issue is examined in detail in my book *The Circadian Prescription*. The gist of it is that your body chemistry during night and day is as different as night and day. A timely intake of food to match differing metabolic needs can make a big difference to the efficiency of your chemistry. Consuming more protein and less carbohydrate in the morning and during the day, while saving carbohydrate for the evening, brings about a dramatic improvement in energy and focus in most individuals.

Alkalinization

This is a key step for some individuals wrestling with problems of their gut flora. Alka-Seltzer Gold (without aspirin, an ingredient in regular Alka-Seltzer) is just a combination of sodium and potassium bicarbonate. Taking it helps your body stay a little alkaline, counteracting the tendency to become too acid when you are feeling sick. The dose is one to two tablets in water, three to four times a day, not on a very full stomach. Consuming the juice of one lemon or a tablespoon or so of apple cider vinegar accomplishes the same thing by a somewhat more indirect method. The citric acid in the lemon juice and the acetic acid in the vinegar are each metabolized in your liver in ways that release bicarbonate and water as the end products of metabolism, as opposed to the carbon dioxide and water released by sugars and oils. The paradox of consuming obviously acid foods to produce a more alkaline state in your body is just one among many causes of confusion for people seeking to sort out the mysteries of pH, the scale by which acidity is measured. You can easily test your response to efforts to stay more alkaline by purchasing Nitrazine or pHydrion paper from your pharmacist. Moistened with a drop or two of urine, the paper will change color to show whether your urine is more acid (below 7) or alkaline (above 7). The scale on which pH is measured, like the

Richter scale for earthquakes, is a log scale, meaning that the distance between whole numbers is a tenfold difference. Thus, a pH of 6 is ten times more acid than 7, and 100 times more acid than 8. High numbers are more alkaline; low numbers are more acid. Your stomach pH is about 1, your blood is 7.4, vinegar is about 3, lemon juice is 1, and a teaspoon of baking soda in water is about 8. Your stools normally range between 6 and a little over 7.

If regular consumption of lemon juice leads to a consistent urine pH above 7, then you will have an easier time restoring your bowel flora to normal. It is not at all clear why this is so and, as far as I can tell, the point has never been proven in a controlled study.

The connection between alkalinization and maintenance of a healthy flora in the intestine has nothing to do with stool pH, which, unlike the acid/base balance of your blood and other body fluids, is not controlled by your own chemistry. Stool pH is a reflection of the metabolic activity of the germs that inhabit your large intestine. Your digestion affects their balance, so that if you are unable to digest certain sugars—lactose, for example—your stools will eat the lactose that passes undigested from your small intestine to the large intestine and produce acid. If, on the other hand, you fail to digest protein, your lower intestinal germs will feast on that and produce ammonia, which turns your stools alkaline. Even if your digestion is perfectly good, an imbalance of germs provoked by taking antibiotics or from a too-sweet diet may push stool pH up or down, depending on the dominance of certain germs among the hundreds of different kinds that inhabit your gut. If your bowel germs get out of balance, your immune system and body chemistry seem to have very limited leverage in restoring normal balance. For reasons that are not clear, alkalinization does seem to help in that process.

If you have a history of calcium-containing kidney stones, you should be cautious with alkalinization because an acid urine keeps calcium salts in solution and alkaline urine permits crystals to form. A supplement of magnesium and vitamin B_6 may keep calcium stones from forming. If you have a history of uric acid stones, the acid-alkaline situation works the other way. Alkaline urine, such as obtained with lemon juice, helps keep uric acid stones from forming.

Getting Rid of Parasites

If a stool examination turns up a parasite, getting rid of it is a high priority. The term *parasite* refers to one living being living at another's expense, so it may be applied to creatures of all sizes and species, even human, when broadly interpreted. When it comes to stools, it refers collectively to two completely different sizes and types of creatures: worms and certain single-celled organisms (but not yeasts or other fungi, or bacteria). Because the line between fungi and these single-celled organisms is pretty thin, the term *parasite* is arbitrary and a little vague. A big worm (such as a roundworm) in the toilet or even a fingernail clipping–sized pinworm on a child's stool produces a squeamish response to those of us living in modern cultures, in which such infestations are not everyday occurrences as they used to be nearly everywhere in the not-too-distant past. There is no disagreement among doctors that worms, if found, should be eradicated. There is a growing body of evidence, according to some doctors, that the eradication of worms from most of the population has been associated with a higher incidence of allergies and autoimmune diseases. It is as if anti-worm immune defenses left idle have caused mischief by attacking innocent targets in our diet and environment to produce allergy and in our own tissues in the form of autoimmune conditions.

A bigger disagreement exists among doctors from two camps with regard to "minor" intestinal amoebae. These have the long double names of biological classification: genus and species. Blastocystis hominis is the most common. Others are Dientamoeba fragilis, Entamoeba hartmanni, Endolimax nana, Entamoeba coli, and Balantidium coli. Well-trained doctors often take the view expressed in textbooks of parasitology that these germs do not generally cause severe problems, especially when compared with their virulent cousins Entamoeba histolytic and Giardia lamblia. In a tropical medicine setting, such as Africa, where I practiced from 1966 to 1968, these minor parasites were indeed overlooked and left untreated because they were common and could not compete for attention with other, more virulent, amoebas and worms. I returned to the United States with that attitude until the current medical literature, the advice of colleagues such as Warren Levin, M.D., and experience with my own patients taught me the value of eradicating these parasites. That value often has little to do with bowel symptoms but touches on a variety of problems that can be evoked by an immune system that is unhappy about a foreign presence in your body and fights with only partial success to get rid of it. Fatigue, malaise, rashes, night sweats, headaches, and a long list of vague problems disappear with the elimination of parasites.

For a number of years, I had success in using natural remedies, such as those derived from citrus seed and wormwood (Artemisia annua). In the late 1980s, I encountered more and more treatment failures. (Treatment success is defined by three parasite-free stool exams following treatment.) Natural remedies remain an option, but I now turn to one of the following protocols as a first line of defense:

1. Bactrim or Septra (sulfamethoxazole and trimethoprim) plus Humatin (paromycin) for fourteen days. I use an adult dose of one Bactrim DS or Septra DS twice daily and Humatin 250 mg four times daily for fourteen days. When prescribing this treatment, I also make sure to provide an antifungal medication to avoid the fungal overgrowth that often accompanies antimicrobial drugs. (Paromycin works by killing normal flora as a way of starving out the parasites.)

2. Yodoxin (diiodohydroxyquin) 650 mg three times daily for two weeks. Yodoxin has the disadvantage of being slightly more toxic—though I have never seen toxicity in any person in the past twenty years—but it has the advantage of being antifungal as well as antiparasitic. (It is the active ingredient in Vioform, a cream widely used by doctors for treating yeasty rashes.)

Getting Rid of Yeasts

If a stool examination turns up yeasts or other fungi, most physicians will tell you that yeast is a normal inhabitant of the human intestine and that there is no scientific evidence of benefits from treating it in a person with a normal immune system. Eradicating normal intestinal yeast is not feasible. So, unlike other germs such as TB, parasites, and strep, where zero is the right number after treatment, yeast treatment involves reducing the number to a point of tolerance, which differs from one person to another. If you choose to seek a trial of therapy as treatment for intestinal yeast—that is, take the treatment and see if it convincingly helps your symptoms—then these are your options.

Saccharomyces Boulardii

Twenty years ago my colleague, Leo Galland, M.D., told me about this "yeast against yeast." I was incredulous that individuals with a yeast problem could benefit from taking something that seemed to me to be almost certain to provoke an allergic reaction the way that brewer's yeast and yeasty foods often do. Dr. Galland trusted the reports of French doctors who routinely used S. boulardii and we started prescribing it in our practices. It has the advantage of being both "natural" and readily available without a prescription. Natural is no guarantee that it is safer than pharmaceuticals. After all, taking S. boulardii is like swallowing the pharmaceutical company. S. boulardii manufactures antifungal substances. Once swallowed, it arrives in your intestine where it sets up shop, blooms, and makes two substances: lactic acid and yeast-killers. If you stop taking it, it wakes up one day and realizes that it is not in its native habitat, which, of all things, is the surface of a lichee nut. At that point, or soon thereafter, it clears out of your gut. If it has done its two jobs well, it will have promoted the reestablishment of good flora while reducing the numbers of bad yeasts to a manageable level. If you are using a stool culture to monitor success, you should wait for about a month. The lab cannot distinguish between S. boulardii and S. cerevisiae (baker's and brewer's yeast). If, after taking S. boulardii, the lab reports isolating S. cerevisiae, it is very likely the lingering S. boulardii has been mistaken in the lab for S. cerevisiae.

If you have had a stool culture that is positive for yeast, you and your health practitioner may be curious to see if it is gone after treatment. So go ahead and repeat the culture, but do not take the results too seriously. Stool cultures are simply not decisive. By this I mean that they do not provide evidence sufficient by itself to indicate treatment, predict the outcome of treatment, or judge the success of treatment. I have seen hundreds of patients with stool cultures that failed to show yeast but responded unequivocally to antifungal treatment. I have seen many other patients who had high levels of fungal organic acids in their urine—sure evidence of the presence of yeasts—but whose stool cultures were negative. Conversely, I have seen many patients whose yeast cultures were strongly positive for one or more species of yeast yet failed to produce the signature organic acids in their urines. In other words, lab tests can be helpful when positive for yeast in the gut, but they are not decisive. The decisive test is a trial of antifungal medication. About a third of patients fail to have any response to S. boulardii. Does that mean that they will fail to respond to another antifungal medication? No.

An initial course of S. boulardii should last about three weeks at a dose of three capsules daily for an adult. If you don't see any encouraging effects at that point, it is time to consider other options.

Nystatin

In terms of potential toxicity, nystatin is the next step up the ladder. You should take it in its pure powder form and allow it to spend some time in your mouth before swallowing it because the mouth is a favored place for yeast colonization. Moreover, because it is not absorbed into the blood, you must take it frequently. Most medications, once swallowed, pass into your blood where their levels reach a peak after an hour or so and then begin to dwindle as they are detoxified in your liver and/or excreted in your urine. The effect is like a tide, rising for a period of time, and then subsiding. Taking nystatin, however, is like throwing apples into a river. They bob on downstream, where at any one point you can see them go by, but then they are gone until someone throws in some more apples. If you have yeasts in any part of your digestive tract, from your mouth on down, then the nystatin will be effective only while it is passing by. After that, yeasts that were not killed can reproduce and reestablish their colonization until the next dose of nystatin comes by.

Nystatin is without any significant toxicity because it stays within the bowel. In twenty-five years of prescribing nystatin to thousands of individuals I have never seen a toxic reaction. I have, however, seen die-off reactions. They presumably occur when the toxins released from dying yeasts provoke the symptoms under treatment and, sometimes, symptoms that are new to the patient. S. boulardii and nystatin provoke the worst die-off reactions, which may begin within hours of taking the first dose or after a few weeks of treatment. The reactions may last for similarly unpredictable periods of time. Following the dietary recommendations listed above and by all means avoiding constipation will minimize the chance of a major die-off reaction.

If you experience die-off reactions (flare of just about any symptom), take activated charcoal, which comes in tablets or capsules over the counter at the drugstore. The dose is about four capsules per day. Do not take it with food or any medication, including nystatin, because it absorbs everything it contacts. The idea is to absorb the toxins that are being released. Activated charcoal is a simple and harmless remedy that is used in poison control. It is administered to soak up whatever poisons a person may have just ingested. It is also an ingredient in over-the-counter remedies for gas. In autistic children whose die-off reactions may take the form of terrifying regression and aggressively violent and irritable behavior, it is amazing to see how well activated charcoal works to quench the reaction. Its effectiveness reinforces our understanding of the mechanism of the die-off reaction: the release of toxins, which the charcoal absorbs to quiet the reaction. Three weeks at a dose of ¼ teaspoon (1,000,000 units) of nystatin four times daily should produce a convincing effect. If it doesn't, then it is likely time to consider other options. If you get a good effect, it can be maintained safely for weeks to months if symptoms return with discontinuation. Enormous doses of nystatin have worked when the normal dose fails, so, if you are able to tolerate the taste, you may consider one to three teaspoons four times daily as an alternative to trying the potentially more toxic systemic antifungal medications I will discuss next.

Other Antifungals

Individuals whose immune systems are faulty because of genetic problems; infections, such as human immunodeficiency virus (HIV); medication, such as steroids and anticancer drugs; and underlying medical conditions such as diabetes are especially susceptible to yeast infections. Prior to the 1980s, when the drug Nizoral (ketoconazole) came on the market, the drugs to combat severe yeast infections were quite toxic and doctors of my generation came to view antifungal medications other than nystatin with apprehension. I find that there is a lingering fear of antifungals on the part of many doctors. "Liver damage" is the phrase that comes straight from the fine print of the package inserts for Nizoral, Diflucan (fluconazole), Sporanox (itraconazole), Lamisil (terbinafine), and others that are coming on the market. In thousands of patients for whom I have prescribed Diflucan and Sporanox I have seen not a single adverse reaction. I monitor "liver profile" tests and stop the medication if I see a rise above normal. In the 1980s, I had two patients on Nizoral whose liver function tests became rapidly abnormal as they developed jaundice. They recovered completely after stopping the medication. Recently a patient had a reaction that transiently affected her kidney function within two days of starting Lamisil. According to the manufacturer, hers was a 1-in-40,000 long shot.

As ominous as "damage" sounds when coupled with any organ in the body, you need to keep in mind that the area most susceptible to damage and difficult to repair is your intestinal flora. A short course, or even a single dose, of antibiotics can alter your intestinal germ population in ways that are enduring and stubbornly resist restoration. Antifungal medications may be necessary in that repair because they are the most effective way of ridding the unwanted overgrowth of fungi. The very small risk associated with these drugs is well balanced by the enormous benefits many individuals achieve.

The basic question is "Are some or all of my symptoms caused by a yeast problem?" No lab test will give a decisive answer. A trial of antifungal medication will do so only if the fungus in question is sensitive to that particular medication. So what if S. boulardii fails to work? Maybe there was no yeast problem. Or maybe the S. boulardii just was not the right remedy for the particular strain(s) of yeasts involved.

The lab gives us some help when tests identify yeasts in a stool culture. Sensitivity testing can tell us which antifungal medications and natural remedies suppress the yeast most effectively in the test tube. These tests are a very good, but still imperfect, guide. I have started patients on Diflucan pending the outcome of a culture only to discover that their yeast was strongly resistant to Diflucan. When I called them to make a change in the treatment, I found that their symptoms had cleared so quickly and completely as to leave little doubt that the Diflu-can had done the job. The final answer to the question I have posed is that you can never be sure that you have done everything possible to diagnose a yeast problem if you focus only on its response to a series of treatments. The best you can do is to work your way through the antifungal medications as swiftly as possible, monitoring the appro-priate laboratory tests to minimize risk. This can be a very tedious pro-cess even if you adhere to a schedule of about three weeks on each antifungal. Each failure to achieve the expected results dims your hopes and makes you feel as if you are wasting your time with expensive and potentially risky health gambles. Still, I believe that failure to see this diagnostic process through may miss a miracle. Let me give you an example.

Alina Carroll had been symptom-free for seven years after allergy injections brought her fierce eczema under control. Measles immun-ization was required when she enrolled in an adult education program at a local college, so she had received a measles, mumps, and rubella immunization in June, followed by a second measles virus shot in July. Six weeks later, her eczema flared, leaving her covered with crusting, oozing lesions. She was so itchy that she couldn't sleep and could barely think.

Because eczema is so often an expression of yeast allergy, I wanted to be sure to cover that possibility even though she had not taken antibiotics in the previous months, had not been pigging out on car-bohydrates or yeasty foods, and had not had a heavy exposure to mold. Her only risk factor had been the immunizations, which could have been involved by affecting the division (so-called TH1) of her immune system that deals with antiviral and antifungal immunity.

I asked her to try a yeast-free diet, which had previously been help-ful for her condition. Meanwhile, she took a course of nystatin, fol-lowed by Diflucan, then by Nizoral, and finally by Lamisil. Three weeks of each adds up to twelve weeks—a very long time if you are going out of your mind with itching and having to go to work every day with your skin a mess.

We had been considering other issues including her need for increased doses of omega-3 fatty acids, the potential benefits of primrose oil (a source of the omega-6 fatty acid, gamma-linolenic acid), and the possibility that the immunizations may have triggered a food sensitivity. I still felt that she might have a yeast problem. But I felt guilty proposing that she try yet another antifungal medication in the dying hope that it would be the answer. We had tried all of the antifungal drugs in common use except Sporanox (itraconazole), which I had been shy of recommending because of its possible side effect of causing a skin rash—hardly what she needed to add to her problems. I let her know that I had never seen such a side effect in hundreds of patients treated with Sporanox. She elected to go for it. Within forty-eight hours, she was on her way to recovery, and a few days later she was sleeping well and free of itching. It was a close call, and one among many similar lessons about not giving up on a reasonable suspicion. Her course of treatment over the next months and years made it clear that antifungal treatment had indeed been the key to success. Her story illustrates the point that the most difficult medical decisions are not what to do next, but when to quit on a reasonable line of thinking when it does not seem to be paying off. I can think of no other area of clinical medicine where this point is more apt than in the pursuit of yeast problems as the cause of mysterious chronic symptoms. When no laboratory test is decisive, the patient is the best lab. When the patient is the best lab, my patient and I should have a mutual understanding of the possible benefits of not quitting prematurely on a diagnostic trial. The protocol I now use for diagnostic trials of antifungal medications involves a two-week treatment at the usual recommended dose, a blood test to check liver function while proceeding with ten days at double the dose. Failure to achieve a significant change in symptoms, indicating that we are in the right ballpark, is taken as an indication to try the next antifungal in the lineup. Success in the form of a convincing response of symptoms provides the option of continuing with the medication, raising the dose further (while monitoring liver, and, with Lamisil, kidney function), and waiting for a plateau in improvement before finding the lowest effective dose (maybe none, if the job has been finished) that maintains health.

I learned about dosage of antifungal medications from Dr. Orian Truss who sometimes prescribed several teaspoons daily of oral nystatin powder to patients who had had no success with the normal dose of ¼ teaspoon four times daily. The usual admonition that "more is not better" is not so true with medications aimed at germs as it is with medications such as painkillers, which are aimed at your own chemistry. My patients taught me that double, triple, or quadruple the dose of the systemic antifungals can work remarkable results when ordinary doses fail. Chuck Franklin, for example, had a stubborn case of psoriasis, which in some people responds miraculously to antifungal medications. I was pleased when he returned for a follow-up visit with his psoriasis cleared up and recommended that he continue taking 200 mg daily. "Oh, but I am taking 600 mg daily," said Chuck. "My wife said that I should just keep increasing until it worked, and as soon as I took 600 mg, it worked like magic, when the lower doses did nothing!" This kind of thing needs to happen only so often to complicate the question of when one has done all one can in going after a yeast problem. It leaves room to consider pushing even higher doses if the treatment should fail to produce the desired results in a person who may have a yeast problem lurking beneath the other symptoms.

What about fungi developing resistance to antifungal medications the same way bacteria regularly do to antibiotics? Naturally, one should always have a reasonable suspicion of the presence of a germ before going after it. In most cases that suspicion is based on finding the germ in question by culturing it, or identifying it microscopically, immunologically, or chemically. Whether treatment is based on laboratory evidence or other reasonable suspicion, it always carries the risk the germ in question will become resistant to the drug and harder to deal with. This is ever more likely with antibacterial drugs than with antifungal drugs. Bacteria make their way in the world by reproducing rapidly with a kind of genetic looseness that gives each new generation a shot at producing individuals who can thrive in an environment the rest of them find difficult. In other words, bacterial strategy is to outmultiply and outmutate the competition. Fungi are much more complex creatures and are as different from bacteria as a kangaroo from a cabbage. Fungal strategy is more dependent on poisoning its competition than on mutation. While many strains of yeasts are resistant to one or another antifungal medication—a point that justifies trying one after another before quitting—they are not as likely to become resistant during treatment of a person or a population as are bacteria.

Antibacterials

When your gut flora is disturbed, the most common and accessible problem is the overgrowth of yeasts. When antibiotics wipe out the good bacteria, they are also replaced by the overgrowth of bad ones. The names of various undesirable bacteria may turn up on your stool culture report along with, if requested by the practitioner, a report of resistance and sensitivity to various antibacterial medications. If one of these germs turned up instead in a urine culture as the cause of a bladder infection—as they often do—then giving the appropriate antibiotic would be the standard thing to do. Not so with bowel germs, especially considering that antibiotics probably unbalanced them to begin with. Some individuals persist with the same bad bacteria over the course of repeated stool cultures, while the stool cultures of other patients keep shifting to show various undesirable bacteria. In either case, what you are seeing on a stool culture report of bacteria is the tiniest tip of an iceberg. Recall that there are up to 500 different kinds (species) of bacteria inhabiting your gut. The vast majority of these germs are anaerobic, meaning that they thrive in the absence of oxygen. None of these are isolated by regular culture methods, yet they are among the leading suspects as the cause of toxic or immunologic reactions.

Any effort to rearrange your gut flora by killing bad germs with the hope of restoring balance by taking in good germs would probably have to begin by reducing the numbers of bad anaerobes. In some instances, this does work. Here are some examples:

1. If your urine organic acids reveal high levels of di-hydropropionic acid (DHPPA), taking an antianaerobe antibiotic works promptly to bring the level down to normal.
2. Studies of autistic children with high levels of DHPPA treated with metronidazole (Flagyl) show transient clinical improvement in behavior and cognition.

3. Some individuals with complex chronic illness accompanied by a history (antibiotics), and lab data (abnormal pH, short-chain fatty acid distribution and culture) suggesting abnormal bowel flora may benefit from a course of a combination of two antibiotics that wipe out a major segment of bowel flora. These are gentamycin and vancomycin. Doctors usually use gentamycin intravenously in a hospital setting for treating dire infections. Taken orally, like nystatin, it does not enter the bloodstream. It kills many kinds of bowel germs at an adult dose of 160 mg five times daily for three days. When combined with vancomycin 250 mg five times daily, it will produce essentially odorless, loose bowel movements by the third day. At that point consuming large doses of probiotics and an antifungal medication offers some hope of restoring a healthy flora, while relieving symptoms that were produced by a toxic bowel.

Here is an example: Polly Karlin was bothered for years by chronic persistent burning and pain in her urethra, the one-inch passage from the bladder to the outside. Her urologist had dilated her urethra without the expected benefit, and numerous cultures had failed to implicate a germ in her urethra or bladder. She and I investigated a number of possible factors that could have triggered inflammation in her bladder. These included an overgrowth of yeast in her intestine and sensitivity to foods. Finally I suggested that she might have a problem with bacteria—not germs in her bladder, but bladder sensitivity to the chemicals produced by bowel bacteria. These chemicals carried through the blood and filtered into the urine might be her bladder's irritants. After three days of gentamycin and vancomycin aimed at killing off a whole slew of bowel germs, she suddenly became free of this symptom. Because oral gentamycin and vancomycin do not enter the bloodstream or urine, but pass through the bowel where their effect is to kill off both normal and abnormal flora, the implication of her success was that her urethra had become sensitized to substances produced in her bowel by bad bacteria.

Another example of inflammation caused by a strange reaction to bowel germs is arthritis. Two common bowel germs (Klebsiella and

Proteus) have been shown to provoke in some people antibodies that react with their joints to produce inflammation of the spine (ankylosing spondylitis, which progresses to make people bend like a question mark) or other joints (rheumatoid arthritis).

I do not mean to suggest that all causes of chronic arthritis or cystitis are caused by such sensitization. Nor does my experience suggest that such sensitization only causes urinary symptoms or arthritis. On the contrary, I believe that immunologic and toxic responses to bowel germs are worth considering when evaluating complex chronic health problems. We may not, one hopes, return to the days of frequent enemas as a means of cleansing the bowel, but the pendulum is swinging back to recognition of the importance of bowel hygiene in understanding chronic health problems.

For a full understanding of the scientific research underlying my clinician's take on the subject, read *The Second Brain* by Michael Gershon, Ph.D. It is a brilliant explication of the following paraphrase of his writing: "If you are seeking the cause of harm to the brain or other tissues of the body, you need not necessarily find a harmful substance in the brain or other tissues. It is sufficient that a substance harms the gut, which by its nerve-connection to the rest of the body, can evoke harm elsewhere."

5

Food as Toxin

LYDIA DVORAK WAS a fellow member of the Yale Medical School faculty, but I probably would never have met her if she did not live across the street. In the thirty years that have elapsed since the time of the story I am about to tell she has become a full professor and a leading expert in her field of psychology and molecular biology. When we were both junior faculty members, she and her husband came over for dinner, and she told me her headache story. She was pregnant with her first child and had developed, for the first time in her life, absolutely crushing headaches. They were the kind of headaches that left her unable to leave a darkened room and were literally blinding, with partial loss of vision. The nausea and vomiting that accompanied the headaches did not seem to have to do with morning sickness but felt to her as if she were trying to eject some kind of poison from her body. Her obstetrician delivered the children of many Yale doctors and other professors, including my own first child, and was particularly thoughtful and skilled. After carefully listening to Lydia's story he identified her problem as migraine and implied very strongly that having a Ph.D. and a baby might be producing some inner conflict that expressed itself as headache. Lydia responded with a strong expletive, fled the doctor's office, and headed two blocks down the street straight to the medical library. Even in those days, before computer searches, she turned up the literature on food migraine within a couple of hours and came up with her own diagnosis. She immediately abandoned the New York State cheddar cheese habit that she had acquired for the sake of getting good protein for her fetus, and her headaches stopped.

There is nothing wrong with New York State cheddar cheese. That is, unless you happen to share Professor Dvorak's sensitivity to tyramine, a natural substance produced in the aging of various cheeses and other foods such as red wine and chocolate. Sensitivity to tyramine is just that, a sensitivity, not an allergy. This is, in my opinion, a silly distinction that still carries a lot of weight in my profession. In general, doctors take sensitivities quite seriously. They are especially careful about drug sensitivities or allergies. However, many doctors, like laypeople, are very skeptical about food sensitivity.

I Become a Believer

Milton Senn was chairman of the Department of Pediatrics and director of the Yale Child Study Center when I first met him. I was an undergraduate at Yale and lived in Davenport College, one of the residential colleges where faculty members might meet with undergraduates over lunch. Dr. Senn was a large, gracious man of Scandinavian origin with bushy eyebrows and a gentle warmth that babies could recognize at a glance and that seemed unsuited to the highly competitive medical school faculty where Dr. Senn thrived. Dr. Senn retired just before I became an intern in pediatrics, which did not inhibit me from seeking his advice and friendship, especially years later when I was asked to become director of the Gesell Institute. Dr. Senn had replaced Dr. Gesell at the time of Dr. Gesell's retirement from the directorship of the Yale Child Study Center, and Dr. Senn had taken that institution on a new, psychoanalytically oriented path.

When I was asked to direct the Gesell Institute, I asked Dr. Senn's advice and he gave his blessing to my effort, even though it was clear that I would continue the Institute's orientation toward biological aspects of development, even expanding the notion to include a medical practice that included adults as well as children. A few years later Dr. Senn became my patient and, in the course of taking his history, he told me the following story.

Not long after coming to Yale, Dr. Senn and his wife consulted their pediatrician concerning problems their baby was having with her skin, sleep, and mood. Dr. and Mrs. Senn were quite convinced that the baby was allergic to eggs. Her problems were severe, though she didn't eat large amounts of eggs. The pediatrician was skeptical and expressed some impatience that a professor of pediatrics and chairman of the department, for that matter, should entertain such a diagnosis as a hidden egg allergy. "Actually," said Dr. Senn at the time of their consultation, "we think she is so sensitive that she cannot even be tested." The pediatrician said "Nonsense," or words to that effect, and proposed an oral challenge of a small amount of egg. The amount was negotiated so that the resulting quantity was one-eighth of a teaspoon of egg white diluted in a quart of water, of which a teaspoon was offered to the baby. Shortly thereafter, she came within an inch of dying from anaphylactic shock. After she was resuscitated, the pediatrician conceded that she was, indeed, a very allergic child.

Here was a stimulus quite different than a tick bite in the ear canal, a reaction to poorly detoxified estrogen, the negative effect of alcohol or other yeast toxins in a person with altered gut function or flora, or the quirky toxicity of tyramine in cheddar cheese. This was just the tiniest bit of a perfectly healthy food, and it was nearly as lethal as the most toxic of substances. How can one person be nearly poisoned by a food that nourishes another? The whole process is so mysterious and physiologically perverse that it gets pushed aside in the training of doctors, who prefer to deal with situations that they can control. In my own training, my chairman (Dr. Senn's successor), Dr. Charles Davenport Cook, took a dim view of allergy and discouraged me from taking any interest in it whenever the subject came up of my own severe allergy to cats. Dr. Cook did encourage me to be interested in nutrition, but allergy was not considered a respectable pursuit. The pediatric allergy clinic at Yale was the only specialty clinic that was still under the leadership of practicing pediatricians from the New Haven community as opposed to full-time academics who, by the early 1960s, had come to dominate medical education in all of the major medical schools.

Except for the little I had learned from my own suffering with hay fever and cat-induced asthma, I knew little about allergies. I completed my training in pediatrics and, after a year as chief resident at Yale, I spent two years on the full-time faculty as an assistant professor of medical computer sciences working in the Department of Obstetrics and teaching in pediatrics. When I went into practice in 1971 as a family practitioner and pediatrician, I believed that allergy, especially food allergy, was inconsequential and that lack of knowledge of it would not affect my ability to do everything I could for my patients.

I started out as one of four primary care physicians in the first health maintenance organization in the Northeast, before the term HMO was in use. At the time we had to be fairly well-staffed even though patient enrollment was just beginning, so I had plenty of time to spend with patients, a habit that remains the backbone of my practice. Frequently, during relatively unfocused conversations with patients, I learn helpful clues that open new avenues for solving their problems. I listen a lot. I take complete medical histories of the kind I was taught to do as a medical student and intern. Medical students (who work on the medical wards of the hospital as clinical clerks) are required to write up a complete history and the findings of a complete physical exam of patients assigned to them when they are admitted to the hospital.

However it is organized, the traditional content of the history is supposed to begin with a statement concerning the presenting problem, usually quoting the patient's own words to describe what is wrong after a terse demographic statement: Mrs. Smith is a thirty-seven-year-old, divorced, white paralegal and mother of two children who presents with "severe headache." After a description of the onset, duration, periodicity, aggravating and alleviating factors, and associated symptoms, the medical student is expected to record past illnesses, past injuries, allergies—especially to medications—drug usage, social and family history, and what is known as a review of systems, an inventory of complaints referable to the respiratory system, digestive system, reproductive system, etc. As the student progresses up the ladder and eventually becomes a physician in his or her own office, he or she generally adopts the hasty, illegible, and incomplete methods of the top of the hierarchy.

Dr. Lawrence L. Weed, now an emeritus professor at the University of Vermont Medical School, came along in the 1960s to take some initial giant steps in teaching changes in record-keeping as well as the thinking that goes with it. The method in place at the time was to cap the history and physical exam described above with a discussion of the differential diagnosis in which the student explicitly describes his or her choices among the various diseases that could be present considering the history, physical findings, and initial laboratory results. The value of the exercise is that it helps the student learn to discard the irrelevant and focus on the relevant facts in arriving at a parsimonious conclusion concerning the patient's condition. Dr. Weed wrote and spoke eloquently and at times scathingly about the tendency of the diagnosis-oriented approach to overlook problems that were either important to the patient's overall health (e.g., getting divorced) or could have crucial ancillary importance to the treatment of the present diagnosis (e.g., underlying diabetes). His problem-oriented approach encourages physicians to list all the patient's difficulties, abnormalities, and situations that can be described as problems without having to dignify them as diagnoses. The approach leads to thoroughness and it particularly discourages the medical tendency to lose track of details in a patient's story that are deemed irrelevant because they do not constitute criteria for arriving at a diagnosis.

As I learned a tolerance for tracking "irrelevant" details, I also learned patience with "irrelevant" questions posed by patients as they struggled to sort out the meaning of problems seen from their perspective. Such questions usually begin with the word *could*.

When I started out low in the hierarchy as a primary care physician—or provider, as we are now called—I was particularly troubled by my patients' questions that began with *could*. The more time I spent listening to my patients' stories, the more trouble I had answering with the timesaving word *no*, which would be easier to utter if I were focused on making a diagnosis rather than on understanding all the problems.

The questions often came up when I was trying to take a complete medical history including, "Tell me about past illnesses, injuries, allergies, occupational exposures, and medications you have taken." More often than I expected, my patients indicated in their reply to the allergy query that there were foods they avoided in order to prevent symptoms. Often patients had suffered for an extended period before making the connection between the foods they ate and their symptoms. If I had just heard that a patient avoided foods from the nightshade family (tomato, potato, peppers, eggplant, tobacco) in order to remain free of joint pain, I wondered what to tell the next patient who asked, "Could my joint pain have anything to do with my diet?"

The stories I heard came from completely reasonable and sane people, and when they differed from pronouncements in heavy medical texts that said, for example, that food allergies are rare, I tended to believe the collective voice of my patients. The more I believed my patients, the more difficulty I had giving a flat *no* to questions for which the answer might better be, "It is not likely, but it is possible, so we should check it out." Sometimes, the way to check out the likelihood of allergy was pretty obvious. For example, Hillary Tuckerman became wildly hyperactive when given ampicillin for her earache. Giving an antibiotic to a nine-month-old infant usually relieves pain very promptly.

I had never heard of ampicillin causing an infant to climb the walls, yet Mrs. Tuckerman said that Hillary had turned into a "wild, raving animal," screeching and clawing the air, her bedding, her hair, and her mother about an hour after getting her first dose of the drug. Roused from sleep in my on-call room, I was faced with Mrs. Tuckerman's question, "*Could* Hillary be having a sort of psychotic reaction to the penicillin?" One thing I knew was that the family of penicillin drugs did not cause psychotic reactions. There is a temptation to stop listening when you think that the patient's question seems irrelevant. I had, however, long since learned to weigh the short-term rewards of the pillow against the greater rewards of careful listening. This I did as Mrs. Tuckerman speculated, "Could it be the pink stuff they use to color the suspension?" I didn't think so. "They"—the pharmaceutical company—surely knew how to make children's medicine and would not put anything in it that would turn Hillary into a "beast." "Still," Mrs. Tuckerman suggested, "there is Dr. Feingold who says that food coloring can bother some kids, even make them hyper." I had heard of Feingold, but all I knew was that he had written a popular book saying things that were not medically true. At the time I did not understand the distinction between *True* and *true*. It was probably two years after my nighttime conversation with Mrs. Tuckerman, while having tea served by Dr. Feingold in his eleventh-floor studio on North Point overlooking San Francisco Bay, that the difference between *True* and *true* really sank in.

Something is *true* when reasonable people examine the evidence with an open mind and, well informed of all the facts, admit that, for example, some children react to some foods or food additives with changes in mood, behavior, affect, or attention. It took only a few minutes of conversation with Dr. Feingold for me to discover that he was a man of vast clinical experience: nearly fifty years of observing the effects of allergy. He had a critical mind and the forthright approach to saying what he had to say that is often found in people over seventy. A small, salty, agile man with generous eyebrows and a direct gaze, his conclusions, based on decades of experience, seemed so obviously reliable that the benefit of acting upon his truth (that is, suspecting reactions to foods and food additives when the possibility arises) seemed to me clearly to outweigh the risk of ignoring it. His truth has, however, taken a beating on its way to becoming the Truth. He did not publish his research results in a peer-reviewed scientific journal before writing a book that mothers brought to their pediatricians' offices as if it were a missionary's bible wielded before the heathen. Committees, editorials, and grand rounds presentations denounced Dr. Feingold's description of reality, and eventually studies were conducted to prove that he was wrong. While the studies consistently turned up evidence to support his contention, they were published under titles and reviewed under headlines that touted "negative results," meaning that any doctor who chose to ignore Dr. Feingold's notions would have the protection of his colleagues and anyone who asserted even the partial truth of his observations would be considered a heretic. My experience with Hillary was one of several at that time that helped me reconsider some of the dogma of my mainstream training.

I had Mrs. Tuckerman come to the clinic where I took capsules of ampicillin and showed her how to open them and shake out the white powder so Hillary could take it with a little honey or applesauce as a substitute for the pink suspension. Hillary soon recovered from her earache without any side effects from the drug. Several months later I got a call from Ohio, where Hillary and her mother were visiting Hillary's grandparents. Mrs. Tuckerman wanted my help because

Hillary had again been stricken with an earache. She had been seen by a Dr. Stone, an Ohio pediatrician, who insisted on prescribing a pink suspension. Mrs. Tuckerman had told the doctor about Hillary's previous experience and expressed her concerns about dyes and other food additives, but, according to Mrs. Tuckerman, the doctor ignored her and, with a roll of his eyes, pronounced, "Oh, that's Feingold." Reluctantly, Mrs. Tuckerman agreed to have Hillary take the prescription, and the results were just as she had feared: Hillary was climbing the walls. Now the distraught parent wanted me to intervene and persuade Dr. Stone to prescribe an alternative for her daughter.

Calling Dr. Stone would not be easy for me. I learned Hillary's grandmother and Dr. Stone's mother played bridge together, and that Dr. Stone had been especially kind—getting up at night to actually observe Hillary in orbit. He had been as adamant about his views as he had been sweet to Hillary, and I did not relish speaking with him. I don't like calling strange doctors. I have had some exceptionally bad experiences even though the typical call often works out quite well, more so in the last few years as some doctors have become more tolerant of nondrug approaches to illness. However, at the time of Mrs. Tuckerman's call years ago, I was less experienced and more likely to be scorched by my colleagues' disaffection. The call to Dr. Stone went something like this:

"Hello, Dr. Stone. My name is Sid Baker. My patient, Hillary Tuckerman's mom, asked me to give you a ring. She is very grateful for your care of Hillary, but she is concerned about the possibility that the red dye in the ampicillin is causing a problem. I—"

"Well, Dr. Baker, I appreciate your concern, but I think we agree that Mrs. Tuckerman is a little overboard with this Feingold thing. I am a pediatrician, so I feel qualified to call the shots at this end," said Dr. Stone, who had taken the term "family doctor" as applied to me by Mrs. Tuckerman to imply that I was not a specialist in his domain. The soft gravel in Dr. Stone's voice let me know that I was speaking to a man many years my senior and one with whom I would have cordially agreed on the importance of breast-feeding or exercise, but we were not to reach agreement on the possibility of individual reactions to food coloring in children's medicines.

He protested by adding, "I'm a small-town doc but I practice scientific medicine. I can't get carried away with every new fad, especially one that is not only unsupported in the peer review journals, but actually has been disproved, according to what I read. I have people here telling me that food colorings, salicylates, and all sorts of other stuff cause this hyperactivity thing, and I just don't see it." Dr. Stone held to the same dogma that I was beginning to shed: Diseases are entities (e.g., "this hyperactivity thing"), and the clinician's job is to identify the disease and then aim therapy at it. If hyperactivity is the "thing" and "they" (peers) say that it is not caused by food additives, then a good doctor waits until "they" figure out what "the treatment" should be, meanwhile resisting any secular challenge to the whole idea of how people get sick; they are the victims of the attack by diseases. I could tell that Dr. Stone was going to yield on the case in point without ever yielding the high ground he had claimed. That was fine with me. I just wanted to get off the phone without having to call Mrs. Tuckerman with news of my defeat.

"Please understand, Dr. Stone, that Mrs. Tuckerman just thought it might be helpful for you to hear from me that Hillary had an identical reaction to the ampicillin that I prescribed for her and she cooled off as soon as we switched to powder from the capsules."

Tension mounted as Dr. Stone pointed out that I had probably not seen this "cooling off" with my own eyes, but, with the last word, he agreed that Hillary could have the powder.

A Resistant Medical Community

In those days I would actually seek out my colleagues at Yale and in the New Haven community and tell them about cases like Hillary's, figuring that my stock was high enough with them to put me on a different footing than I was in conversations like the one I had with Dr. Stone. Within a few minutes of starting such a conversation, however, my colleagues would talk about whatever "disease" my patient had and how there was not any scientifically credible published support for the notion that such-and-such disease is caused by whatever it was that affected my particular patient. I tried to return to the dialogue by saying "Look, this happens. For the sake of argument, accept the fact that on an individual basis patients have peculiar reactions to all sorts of things. Let's talk about how we might apply that to the diagnosis of patients with complex problems that may or may not fit into some particular diagnostic category, but who may have some symptoms provoked by allergic or toxic exposures." I didn't succeed.

My colleagues, especially some of those with the best qualifications, were trained to win arguments. Their most successful tactic is to keep the discussion focused on "the treatment for the disease" and not to accept, for the sake of argument, a shift to observations that could be dismissed as anecdotal. I avoid such conversations now.

The case histories I've recounted are intended to prepare you for a discussion of the "whys and wherefores" of illness. If you understand some basic immunology and biochemistry, you will be better prepared to evaluate the kinds of tests and treatments that your medical doctor, nutritionist, psychiatrist, acupuncturist, personal trainer, coach, homeopath, naturopath, chiropractor, dentist, psychologist, or sister-in-law may recommend in the name of good health. It is not likely that you will be bitten in the ear canal by a tick, but it is certainly possible that some critter, allergen, toxin, bacterium, fungus, or virus will cross your path and lead you to ponder your options for preventing or alleviating the consequences. You may need special lessons to make wise choices among your options when you are told to avoid fat; take antioxidants or minerals; avoid pesticides, hair dye, sugar, coffee, air pollution, medications, sunlight, indoor air, outdoor air, meat, wheat, or long walks in the rain. If you develop chronic or recurring symptoms and wish to be an intelligent participant in your own detective work to sort it out, you definitely need special lessons. The lessons I have to offer will provide a point of view as well as some general principles of immunology and biochemistry that every adult should understand.

A particular point of view and a few basic facts are necessary to understand the threats whose combined effects on your body are usually described as a disease. Understanding how your body handles the substances that enter it is a good place to begin our lessons about the true causes of disease.

You Are *Not* What You Eat

You should not get "eggy" from eating eggs. If you eat an egg, your digestive processes should remove the egginess from the egg's materials so that they enter your bloodstream stripped of any fowl identity and become available for you to impart your own identity on to the stuff that constitutes an egg. Ego is the name of the identity that distinguishes you as a unique creature. When your digestive process works properly it achieves a triumph of your ego over the substances you consume. Otherwise you would accumulate foreign materials whose presence in your structure would undermine your claim to exclusive dominion over your flesh. Not that you would become some sort of omelet of the remnants of your cumulative meals, but your body would be ever less purely "you." You might imagine that Mother Nature would save all of her creatures a lot of work by providing for a certain number of interchangeable parts so that molecules that are costly to synthesize could be moved from prey to predator and save the whole system the expense of their repeated disassembly and reassembly. Instead the system honors individuality so that even cannibal critters must convert their prey into small change and reconstitute the molecules from scratch. The small change is what we call essential nutrients and consists of very small molecules called fatty acids, amino acids, vitamins, minerals, and accessory nutritional factors. If you were to apply the structural analogy to your dwelling, then the construction materials delivered to the building site would be sand or equivalent-sized particles of clay to make cement blocks and bricks, sawdust to make wood, and iron filings to make nails and other metallic parts.

The arrangement—the complete digestion of all the food we swallow—does not always work as it should; in fact, you might get a little eggy each time you eat an egg. It is not just a question of accommodating some vague essence of egg or even the less subtle taint of garlic that enters with your meal and leaves an odor on your breath. Some major molecules—composed of anywhere from two to thousands of subunits—escape digestion, enter your blood, and have to be eliminated. A medium or large molecule that retains its egginess presents a job that is parceled out among functions that include sniffing, identifying, tracking, killing, and disposing of it. So it is with all intruders, be they chemicals, foods, germs, or the toxins produced by germs.

Smell or taste is a first test of a food's edibility. We may develop tastes for certain things, like Stilton cheese and whole fresh fried clams from the fish place down by the wharf, in spite of their unpleasant smell or off taste. For the most part, however, taste is your body's first and conscious effort to identify molecules that may cause mischief and to avoid them. Sometimes the taste is on the edge of acceptability, as was a mouthful of fried clam I purchased in hurried hunger at the end of a long and busy Saturday and brought home to be savored with home-made fixings and a bottle of red wine. "That last mouthful of river bottom belly of a big juicy clam was a little below standard," said my palate. But it was too late now that I had swallowed it. Or was it? Would the taste buds of my stomach give a second opinion? I spent the evening as a spectator to negotiations that were signaled by successive waves of satiety, discomfort, queasiness, and nausea, and I went to bed to sleep it off. Our livers work on the night shift. I knew that as I pre-pared for bed my intestines were asking my liver to taste the clams to see if some accommodation could be worked out. An hour later I was awakened with a strong impression that my liver had come to a deci-sion. The clam was going to be ejected, and my whole meal and bev-erage selection was going with it. The reverse peristalsis that followed was one of the most efficient operations I have ever witnessed in my body. All my efforts to learn to pole-vault or throw the javelin for my track team were miserably awkward compared with the muscular expertise with which my stomach rejected my evening feast of clams and wine with a green salad and French fries.

My palate, stomach, and liver had all tasted the bad clam. My mouth said "ugh" but the clam was not bad enough to spit out. My stomach said, "Let's put this and everything that came with it on hold and see if the liver can handle it," for nearly everything *except* fat passes through the liver—the next stop after the stomach and small intestines. The liver said, "I hate to sacrifice all those good calories, but the molecules in the bad clam are going to cause mischief some-where in the body unless I can detoxify them and I can't." Note that the liver's job was *not* to decide whether the toxins in question would cause cancer. Nowadays when we hear about the safety or toxicity of potentially noxious substances, they are often judged good or bad depending on whether they can be said to cause cancer. That is not the liver's immediate concern when evaluating spoiled food. The liver has to decide whether the toxins would interact badly with any tissue or organ in the body, assuming the liver cannot find a way to deactivate the harmful molecules. This is a particularly delicate assignment when the bad molecules closely resemble good ones. As in all of nature, mimicry is a good way to escape detection; in the case of the bad clam its taste was just a little less acceptable than the ocean bottom taste of acceptable clams.

How Foods Become Toxic

Before tackling the question of how spoiled foods harm the body, which will lead to a discussion of how we can and cannot protect ourselves from them, we need to consider how the bad clam and other substances become toxic. In the case of the clam, it became toxic after it died and it was dead too long when it joined the rest of the clams in my meal. Germs normally found in the clam proliferated after the clam's death and the clam went bad, as we say, at a point after its demise. As the germs multiplied, they released toxins so that when I swallowed them they were crossing the line between unpalatability and poisonousness. The process is quite different from the transmission of clam-related hepatitis. In this case the clam can be quite alive and healthy and remain so until it is part of a meal. The hepatitis clam, however, is harvested from waters contaminated with sewage carrying a virus that is a harmless part of the clam's diet (harmless to the clam, that is). Hepatitis is not food poisoning, but the transmission of a virus.

When we speak of food poisoning, the toxicity is always caused by germs, either ones that infect us or ones that leave their toxins in the food we have consumed. Such is the case of ptomaine poisoning, as when staph germs shed from a food handler find their way into the mayonnaise at the church picnic. The warmth of a summer afternoon is all the staph germs need to thrive in the mayonnaise, covertly spoiling it and, a few hours after the picnic, putting the parishioners on their knees praying for sufficient intervals between alternating obligations to sit or kneel. Human experience with the bad things that germs can do is as long as human experience itself, so the liver does not need lessons in ferreting out ptomaine and other toxins that may escape detection before food is swallowed. Most of the time when food spoils it is because of germs—bacteria and molds—that are present on or in the food when it is fresh and proliferate slowly even in the refrigerator unless the food has been treated to prevent or retard spoilage. The common ways to keep the germs down are heat sterilization and canning, complete drying, or the addition of enough sugar, salt, or acid to poison any germs present and discourage their overgrowth.

So far I have described instances of food, additives, and food-borne toxins causing mischief that comes so soon after eating that the cause-and-effect relationship is not too difficult to figure out. What about the possibility that some foods, additives, and toxins can cause trouble that is sufficiently subtle as to go undetected in the moment, but evoke a bothersome cumulative reaction later on?

What's common to many ailments—asthma, eczema, colitis, chronic cough and mucus, arthritis, psoriasis, dermatitis, and others—is inflammation. Wherever in your body it's going on, the basic chemical reaction of inflammation is the same. Injured cells release informational substances to attract the attention of your body's healing mechanisms. These repair workers are designed to deal quickly with a short-term problem, such as mending a cut, helping you recover from a burn, or fighting off an infection. But sometimes whatever agent is causing the inflammation persists. Or your body's mechanisms for signaling (pain, swelling, redness, and heat) and repairing the inflammation get stuck. Then you're stuck, too, with a chronic inflammation. Diseases described by medical terms ending in -itis or -osis are chronic inflammatory diseases. For anyone suffering from chronic inflammation, food allergy, particularly delayed food allergy, is a consideration.

People in the scientific-medical world spend a lot of time arguing about the precise definitions of words like sensitivity, hypersensitivity, allergy, and intolerance.

Food allergies are reactions to foods that are mediated by your body's immune system. Common wisdom and traditional medical thinking has it that food allergies predominantly affect children and disappear as they get older. The National Institute of Allergy and Infectious Diseases (NIAID) estimates that only 4 or 5 percent of American children and 1 to 2 percent of American adults have food allergy.

Yet as many as one in three adults claims they have reactions to food, and there is clinical and research evidence that the figure is, indeed, closer to 35 percent. So how can we account for the disparity between 2 and 35 percent? If I am giving a talk to a large audience and ask the question "How many of you regularly avoid a food or foods based on your own consistent experience of the food causing pain, itching, fatigue, diarrhea, headache, stuffiness, or other such symptoms?" I usually get a showing of more than 50 percent of those present. It depends, then, on how you define *food allergy*. And one type, delayed food allergy, is controversial.

In this book I use the words *sensitivity*, *hypersensitivity*, *allergy*, and *intolerance* fairly loosely. My bottom line is that some foods just don't agree with some people. But in the scientific-medical world, there's a lot of debate about what a food allergy is. The vehemence of the arguments that take place in medical journals and at medical specialty meetings is striking, more suited to religious or political debates than to scientific discourse. Listening with a commonsense ear, you can detect definite tones of ego, turf, and economics, as well as the understandable difficulty we all have in abandoning a public stance or one we have learned from our professors.

The roots of this intense debate lie in the legacy of the evolution of allergy as a specialty. Just beyond the memory of most practicing physicians today was an era in which allergy was an empirical movement within medicine struggling to attain the high ground of scientific credibility. As recently as the early 1960s, professors at Yale and other medical schools pooh-poohed it. So the field of allergy has evolved with a special thirst for academic respectability that can only be quenched by rigorous standards of proof. The irony is that such standards are particularly difficult to attain when you consider that the biology of allergy is all tied up with individuality. Properly conducted scientific studies that are based on the assumption that all participants are the same with respect to certain variables are especially difficult to conduct in a field in which the very difference between your own and your neighbor's reactions to foods, pollens, mold, and so on is the whole idea.

You are not the same, biochemically or immunologically, as your neighbor or anyone else. And your individuality, particularly with respect to the world of allergies, stems in part from your genetic inheritance and how it plays out in your immune system, which is in charge of accurate recognition of the molecules that enter your body.

Under normal circumstances immune perception takes place below the level of consciousness. So we are less attuned to the ways in which the various mechanisms of the immune system—antibodies, complement, T-cell and macrophage processing, and various cytokines—are orchestrated to recognize a given foreign antigen (germ, allergen, or toxin) and, at times, to bring that recognition to a conscious level with the production of symptoms such as fever, inflammation, itching, or nausea. Still, it's scientifically reasonable to insist that immune mechanisms, like our conscious perceptions, are coordinated in flexible and subtle ways depending on the situation. And it's unreasonable to insist that any one mechanism is the sole reliable mediator of the whole class of immunological experiences known as allergy. In other words, you might recognize your friend by his face, his voice, the touch of his hand, and his aftershave. When you think about it, you wouldn't specify just one of these particulars as the sole mediator for your perception; you take into account information from all of your senses. Eyewitnessing is considered more reliable than ear witnessing, but we all agree that it is unreasonable to reject any kind of credible evidence as we try to take in the world around us. So it must be with the immune system, which combines its various means of tagging and identifying molecules to come up with action based on their being friend or foe.

Nevertheless, traditional allergists generally accept as true or classic food allergy only those cases where there is a definite, demonstrable (and generally demonstrable under double-blind, controlled conditions) presence of IgE antibodies. These are the same culprits associated with itching eyes when you're around cats or your sneezing fits during hay fever season. Antibodies (or immunoglobulins, hence the Ig) are the shock troops of your immune system, the body's defense department. Using IgE as well as IgG, IgA, and IgM antibodies, the immune system recognizes and keeps track of friendly and unfriendly cells, germs, food molecules, or toxins. Antibodies attach themselves to trespassers (antigens), tagging them so that they'll be visible to the other immune cells that are summoned to your defense.

In the case of so-called classic food allergy, the trespasser is a protein that escapes unscathed from the heat of cooking or your body's digestive process. Once the protein has been tagged, the immune system remembers it. Whenever it reappears, IgE antibodies recognize it, rush in, and trigger other cells to release chemicals such as histamine. The consequences range from an itchy mouth after eating certain fruits and vegetables to a mild stomach upset to a full-scale life threatening anaphylactic meltdown. IgE-based reactions usually occur within an hour of eating the offending foods. They usually involve the skin, respiratory system, or gastrointestinal tract. The claim that only 1 to 2 percent of American adults have food allergies is based on this traditional definition.

But the immune system has other ways besides IgE to perceive and recognize intruders. Most sensitivity to food involves delayed reactions and has to do not with IgE, but with IgG antibodies.

It's a cinch to figure out that you're allergic to strawberries if you get a rash every time you eat them. But it's tricky to pin down a delayed food allergy because there is often no clear-cut cause and effect. You may experience symptoms after two hours, but frequently they don't show up until twenty-four to seventy-two hours after you eat the food in question. Further complicating matters, the symptoms wax and wane. You may eat soy with impunity one day but get diarrhea from it the next three times you indulge. Or your symptoms may be cumulative, occurring only after you've eaten the food a number of times or when you eat a particular combination of foods.

Still, it's worth taking the trouble to sort it out. Delayed food allergies can cause just about any symptom, and chronic illness often involves a state of inappropriate immune vigilance in which food allergy gets involved even if it is not the cause of the problem. For some reason, your immune system can get stuck in high gear, leading to chronic inflammatory symptoms that persist and even worsen long after the initial trigger has gone. When this happens, your immune system may develop an oddly aggressive attitude toward a variety of antigens, including many found in your lunch.

The list of ailments connected with delayed food allergies is enormous: chronic pain, depression, fatigue, joint pain, eczema and dermatitis, celiac disease (gluten sensitivity), headaches, seizures, diarrhea and other gastrointestinal problems, recurrent sinus or ear infections, chronic sinusitis, asthma, coughs, and Ménière's disease. And that's just the tip of the iceberg. "I've identified about 150 medical conditions supported by published scientific literature," says James Braly, M.D., author of *Food Allergy Relief* (Keats Publishing, 2000). What's more, delayed food allergies are an underlying cause or aggravating factor in many chronic illnesses, including autoimmune diseases, fertility problems, difficult pregnancies, rheumatoid arthritis, asthma, inflammatory bowel disease, and other inflammatory ailments. In fact, if you suffer from any chronic condition that doesn't respond to conventional therapy, you may want to consider delayed food allergy.

So how does delayed allergy work? The heart of the problem lies in your gut, or gastrointestinal tract. As I said before, you are not supposed to get eggy from eating eggs. But sometimes proteins or imperfectly digested protein in the form of peptides cross your gut wall into your bloodstream. If they do, your immune system steps up to the plate. Sixty percent of your immune system is centered in your gut, not surprising since the food that passes through your digestive tract and the germs that share your food are the sources of most foreign materials you encounter in the world.

The first line of defense against unwanted molecules from your gut is your IgA antibody, whose major role is protecting your gut wall and other mucosal surfaces. IgA attach themselves to the peptides and, with the help of your liver, direct them back into your gut.

But IgA has its limitations. Fortunately, when this defense mechanism gets overwhelmed, your body has a backup: IgG antibodies. They combine with the peptides and mark them so that macrophages, your body's scavengers, can clean them up.

When an antibody, such as IgA or IgG, combines with the foreign material from your gut, the result is a potentially inflammatory body called an immune complex. Your body has a number of ways involving your liver, spleen, and red blood cells, to clear immune complexes and prevent them from causing damage. These mechanisms help prevent you from reacting strongly every time undigested food materials escape from your gut into your bloodstream.

The trouble starts if these systems get overloaded, thanks to poor digestion or a leaky gut. If, for some reason, your gut wall becomes more permeable, it allows more and larger peptides to escape, which then combine with antibodies to form more and larger immune complexes. And if these immune complexes aren't cleared, they continue to grow and are eventually deposited in tissue.

Many things can cause your gut to become leaky. But the most important reason is overuse of antibiotics. Parasites and other chronic infections as well as alcohol consumption can affect gut permeability. And endurance sports, poor diet, pregnancy, and other periods of physical stress may also play a role.

One of the ironies of the medical profession is that the use of certain medications to relieve symptoms may at the same time make matters worse. For example, rheumatoid arthritis sufferers are regularly told to use NSAIDs (nonsteroidal anti-inflammatory drugs such as ibuprofen, Advil, Motrin, and others). These medications do relieve pain. But they also increase gut permeability and create more immune complexes, which are linked to the development of arthritis in the first place.

So what happens when immune complexes aren't cleared by your body's overworked defenses? Typically, it takes some time for them to build up. But as they do, they cause the symptoms of delayed food allergy.

As the immune complexes float around, they cause inflammation. You may feel achy and feverish, as if you have the flu. Over time, immune complexes deposit themselves in places where there may have already been some damage. They may go to joints, where they become involved with arthritis; to your kidneys, where they may play a role in hypertension; to the blood vessels of your brain, contributing to migraines; or to your lungs, heart, or any other organ. They can go just about anywhere, and this accounts for the wide variability in long-term symptoms. The ways in which you respond to foods also depends, to some degree, on your genetic makeup. One person's immune system may have difficulties with antigens from wheat, while another may be unable to handle milk.

Delayed food allergies don't show up on the traditional skin tests that allergists use. Instead, there's a blood test, called IgG ELISA that measures levels of IgG antibodies to more than 100 foods.

This test doesn't prove that any particular food is causing your symptoms because finding high levels of IgG antibodies to foods doesn't necessarily mean that you are clinically allergic to any one of them. In other words, you can't simply equate high IgG antibody levels with illness. Some people make IgG antibodies but have an efficient clearing mechanism for them. Others may have the same IgG antibody levels, but because they don't clear them as well are more susceptible to developing allergies. What's more, some high IgG levels are cross-reactivities to other antigens, including microbial antigens (e.g., you have a reaction to oysters but have never tasted one), and others are simply immunologic noise.

Still, elevated IgG antibody levels are reliable markers for delayed food reactions, provided they are identified by a lab with a high level of technical expertise. The lab you deal with should help their physician clients occasionally submit split specimens to show that serum from the same specimen produces the same results. The IgG ELISA test results suggest a number of foods—rarely are people allergic to only one—to which you may be reacting. On the list of reactive foods there is likely to be one or more that provoke your symptoms.

If you have done a blood test to identify food allergies, here are suggestions about what to do.

1. **Remember, illness is a signal to change.** Chronic symptoms are a message from your body that you should change something to do with your immune system, your biochemistry, or your life. Sick people have differing capacities to bring about changes that may help, or be the absolute key, to get them well. Some people are very protective of their dietary habits even though such habits are frequently implicated in their illness. When I hear a person declare "I could not possibly give up eating bread" or "How could anyone go without eating things with milk in them—milk is in so many things" I think that I may be hearing from one of the many people whose capacity to change is not up to the challenge that their illness is placing before them. But remember, so far we are talking about a short-term diagnostic change, not a permanent change unless your body tells you that such a change is helpful.

2. **Don't panic.** The test results are very helpful in sorting out symptoms of just about any kind—from seizures to rashes, from diarrhea to depression—but the foods you see marked as "positive" (+) or "reactive" are not to be forever stricken from your menu. This is a diagnostic test, not a treatment recipe, and the only thing you have to do with the results is to try them out for a minimum of five days, and preferably about two weeks, to see if the diagnosis that food sensitivity is causing some of your symptoms is accurate. If so, then you can proceed from there. Only rarely would a person want to consider a prolonged avoidance of all their reactive foods without noticing some definite improvement in symptoms.

3. **Look at the total number.** Allergic people average about a dozen reactive foods. People with "no allergies" (that is, those who are unaware of having reactions to foods, pollens, dust, mold, chemicals, and animal dander) usually have a half dozen or fewer reactive foods. People with lots of allergies tend to have up to two dozen or more reactive foods. If the total number of reactive foods is a dozen or more, it is more likely that the list will reveal the cause of your symptom(s) than if you only have a few reactive foods. You can still have a serious food allergy problem among a small list of reactive foods, but, in general, the more foods you react to on the test the more likely that one or some of them account for symptoms.

4. **"I have never eaten oysters or alfalfa, but my tests say I am allergic to them."** One of the first things people notice when reviewing their test results is any indication of a reaction to a food that they never eat. They are right to be puzzled because one thing we know about the immune system is that it is very specific and it has a very good memory. In principle you should not be positive to foods you have never eaten. But the whole point about the immune system and illness is that mistaken identity is not only the source of puzzles but of trouble. Your immune system may mistake a certain food for something that you have been exposed to (germs, pollens, molds, or even molecules that

are part of your own molecular makeup) and develop an inappropriate reaction. That does not mean that it is easy to interpret a positive test to oysters, say, when you can swear that oysters have never touched your lips, but it is not so simple as to say the test is wrong. (Actually oyster reactivity is often provoked by a cross-sensitivity with bacteria.) The test is not perfect, but your immune system probably makes mistakes more often than the test does!

5. **The test isn't perfect.** This test is very good at providing a list of foods, which, if avoided, will lead to the alleviation of symptoms. The value of the test does not, however, depend on an unvarying correspondence between any particular food and any particular symptom. Such a relationship is for you to work out by trial and error after an initial abstinence from all the foods on the list satisfies you that you are in the right ballpark. There will nearly always be foods on the list that produce no discernible change in your health when you eat them. There may also be foods that you know bother you but that are nonreactive on the test even though you have eaten some from time to time before the test. There are many ways that foods can bother a person. Not all ways have to do with immune mechanisms or with mechanisms for which there is any test. IgG antibodies are a good guide—I think the best there is—but they are not meant to be taken as absolutely decisive as to all the foods that could bother you.

6. **IgG antibodies are a marker, not necessarily the cause of delayed allergies.** Your immune system perceives the world of molecules just as you perceive the world around you by the overlapping use of your several senses. If you go downtown for dinner and a movie, it would be strange for you to describe some good or bad memory of the event only in terms of what you heard, saw, tasted, smelled, or felt. You would normally invoke two or more of your senses to recall a description of the event. Similarly the immune system has many ways of receiving and recording its experience of foods, germs, chemicals, and other events that make up its

experience of the world. The particular blood protein, immune globulin type G or IgG, that forms the basis for the test is only one of several aspects of your immune system's record of its experience. It appears to be particularly important in delayed food hypersensitivities, just as IgE is important in reactions such as hives and swelling that occur immediately after eating a food. I do not believe, however, that IgG is the exclusive mechanism for delayed food reactivity. I know from experiments that I have conducted that it is a very reliable marker for allergy, and that is what counts when it comes to doing detective work on the cause of difficult and mysterious symptoms.

7. **"I just ate a lot of peanuts before the test. . . ."** Whether you do this test immediately after eating a lot of peanuts or some time later does not make much difference in the results. You would have to abstain from a food for months for your IgG antibodies to go away, and even then I know of some instances in which the antibodies persist. We really do not know how long it takes for antibodies to disappear when a particular person abstains from a particular food. We do know that the test is highly reproducible. Dr. John Rebello, laboratory director of Immuno Laboratories in Fort Lauderdale, Florida, constantly performs quality-control measures to show that the test is reliable and reproducible. Many labs have failed at techniques to ensure such reliability and have abandoned the test as not reproducible. Dr. Rebello has devised modifications to the well-known basic technique of the test so that his staff can split a sample and get the same results in each half just as they can show that your test will vary only a little over a period of weeks whether you ate a lot of this or that food or not. There is a popular misconception among doctors that the IgG ELISA "just shows you what you have been eating." If that were true, individuals with the same diet would have the same results, which is far from the case.

8. **What about the pluses?** The difference between a 1+ and a 4+ reaction to a food is not as much as you might think.

Initially a 1+ reaction needs to be considered just as seriously as a possible indicator of a symptom-causing food as does a 4+ reaction. Of course, the degree of reactivity generally correlates with the potential of a food to be the cause of symptoms, but I think it is wrong to ignore 1+ reactions when you are getting started with the detective work. The scoring system can be confusing when comparing two results from the same specimen when a particular food may score 1+ on one and 2+ on the other. This occurs when the numerical results that generate the scores are close to each other but fall on each side of the divide between 1+ and 2+. Let's say that antibodies to egg produce a result of 499 in one test and 501 in the other half of the split specimen. The results are basically the same, but if the cutoff between giving 1+ or 2+ is 500, then they appear to be more different than they are. The biology and technology of this test are tricky. Don't expect perfection, but use the test as a springboard for the final test—a temporary change in your diet.

9. **What about groups?** When several cereal grains (wheat, rye, oat, barley, rice, corn) or beans (legumes) or milk products come up as positive, it strengthens the impression that some or all members of that family are a problem. As an initial measure, however, I usually do not recommend that patients avoid all members of a group if their test to that item is negative while another member of the group is reactive. For example, if a person reacts to lemon but not grapefruit or orange, then I would only ask him or her to avoid lemon but not the other citrus fruits.

10. **So what is the bottom line?** You won't know the final value of this test until you do a trial avoidance of all the foods indicated as reactive (plus any others that you already know bother you). If, after two weeks of strict avoidance of the reactive foods no aspect of your health has changed, then it becomes unlikely that sensitivity to foods on that list plays a significant role in your symptoms. At that point you can simply reintroduce the reactive foods. If you then notice the appearance or occurrence of symptoms whose disappearance

somehow had escaped your notice, then you will have to go back to square one and repeat the two-week avoidance to see what happens. If no change occurs when either avoiding or reintroducing foods, then you can conclude that sensitivity to the tested foods is probably not an issue for you. I say "probably" because of these mitigating factors:

- There are some foods (particularly wheat and other gluten-containing foods and milk products) that may test positive on IgG testing but that, in you, produce effects that are not really allergic but are mediated by mechanisms that take weeks or months for alleviation after avoiding the food(s).

- It is still possible that a period of longer than two weeks will be needed to show an effect. Usually five days is enough. If there are other strong reasons to suspect a given reactive food (such as a history of heavy exposure during periods of stress or a previous history of intolerance during, say, infancy or early childhood), then there may be justification for prolonging the trial of avoiding the food(s) beyond two weeks.

If there is a change in symptoms when you avoid the reactive foods, then you will still not be sure which are the key foods. You still may not be sure how far the symptom relief may go if some symptoms have been relieved and others remain. For example, you may have headaches and joint pain and achieve relief of only the headaches during the two weeks. You should take that as a green light to continue avoiding the foods with the hope that the joint pain relief will follow in due time. After a couple of weeks of symptom relief you may decide to simply continue avoiding all the foods without knowing which ones are guilty. Some people get such wonderful results that they are content to continue avoiding all the reactive foods. Others would like to whittle their list down to discover the key food(s). To do that you must reintroduce foods one at a time allowing about seventy-two hours after beginning to eat the suspected food once or twice daily. If you do not develop any symptom in the seventy-two hours, then it is unlikely that the reintroduced food is the cause of problems and you can keep it in your diet.

If you do develop symptoms, remove the food, wait for symptoms to clear, and then go on to try other foods. Eventually you will develop a list of offending foods. Most people will have to avoid those foods or seek help in becoming desensitized. Some people will be able to eat these foods on a rotation basis, consuming the food only once every five days. The safest thing is to take the food out of your diet for at least six months. The possibility of reintroducing the food at that point varies tremendously from person to person and from food to food.

6

Heavy Metals

Mercury

IN THE 1950s Emily Marshall had worked in a medical school research lab where they floated heart patients on a bed of quicksilver (mercury). The idea was to detect heart problems by measuring tiny body movements generated by the actions of the heart.

Mercury is quick in the sense that it offers little resistance to the movement of a body suspended on its surface. It is dense; lying on its liquid surface leaves one barely immersed. Emily and her coworkers in the research group played with their vat full of mercury as I did as a child when supplied with a few liquid metallic beads from a broken thermometer.

We all tend to become childlike when confronted with the paradoxical properties of quicksilver. A liter (about a quart) of water weighs one kilogram (2.2 pounds). The same volume of mercury weighs thirteen times more. As it is heavy in that sense, so it is light in the sense of its silvery color and its quick movements. Of the metallic elements such as iron, tin, lead, gold, and silver, quicksilver is the only one that is a liquid at room temperature. Like all elements, and like water, its liquid form takes to the air in the form of an invisible vapor. Mercury vapor is a natural part of the earth's atmosphere; every day you breathe in a tiny amount—about one microgram or one-thousandth of a thousandth of a gram. (A quarter teaspoon of water weighs about a gram.)

Emily came to me with an assortment of symptoms for which different doctors had given different diagnostic names. The question of her past mercury exposure only came up when she and I began to scour the possible explanations for her not feeling well. I raised the question of whether the mercury in her dental fillings could be causing any or all of her troubles. This sparked her memory of having worked in the cardiology lab years ago and caused us to wonder if she might be still carrying a lot of mercury in her body.

Emily and her coworkers would have inhaled comparatively huge amounts of mercury vapor. Their exposure came more from the vapor than from sticking their hands and arms into the tub in which the patients were placed for the tests. That's because liquid mercury does not enter the blood or body tissues via the skin or the intestine. Mercury vapor enters the blood via the lungs. You have never worked in a place with huge amounts of mercury vapor in the air. Still, Emily's story will be of interest to you for several reasons.

First, it reveals the long-standing medical tolerance for the use of mercury and an indifference to wondering about where to draw the line between what is safe and unsafe. The cardiologists in charge of the research lab were not concerned about any danger to themselves, their patients, or their staff. In the 1950s, and even later, doctors used mercury-containing medications. One that I remember from my training in the 1960s was Mercuhydrin, an injectable diuretic widely used to treat the water retention associated with congestive heart failure. No one would use it these days because there are safer and more effective diuretics. In those days, though, no one worried much about the toxicity of the medicine because it was used for short-term treatments. The point is that mercury has a long history of medical use, and it is still used today.

Emily's story is also relevant because you very likely have some mysterious symptoms and probably have silver-mercury amalgam fillings in your teeth. Neither you nor your doctor can be quite sure whether mercury is responsible for some or all of your symptoms.

There's one other lesson from Emily's story. Mercury at very low doses may be harmful to one person but not to another. As I mentioned before, there is at least a thousandfold difference in individual thresholds for mercury poisoning; one researcher has measured differences of one millionfold. Knowing how much mercury it takes to poison the average person is of very little help when the average is somewhere within a range that starts at one and goes to one million. No one knows where to draw the line between what we call mercury poisoning and mercury sensitivity. This situation is quite unlike any other toxin or allergen. Emily's exposure, illness, and treatment are difficult to translate into yours because your sensitivity to mercury may be many times higher or lower. If your sensitivity is higher, then you must at least be conscious of mercury as a possibility. Your specific symptoms are not a very good trigger for thinking about mercury because a list of symptoms for low-level mercury toxicity covers just about any complaint you could name. The rule to remember from Emily's story is that you have to think about mercury before doing something about it. The lesson I learned from treating Emily to remove the large amounts of mercury that remained in her body more than forty years after her exposure was that it was not too late to relieve many of her symptoms: fatigue, eczema, irritable bowel, acid reflux, and intermittent urinary urgency and pain.

No one knows exactly how variability in mercury sensitivity works, considering that its range exceeds other differences between people. Surely, one factor is a basic quirk in the biochemistry of sulfur, an element that accounts for much of the stickiness needed to put things together as well as to detoxify, which, you will remember, involves putting good molecules together with toxic molecules for the sake of ushering toxic ones safely from the body. You may recall a news story about a professor at Dartmouth College who died months after touching a particularly toxic form of mercury. She touched only a tiny drop and did so wearing a rubber glove. Her long illness and death must have come about because of a quirk in her ability to detoxify mercury and a domino effect within her chemistry, in which the toxicity was magnified rather than minimized over time as would usually be the case.

Not knowing how sensitive any given person may be is just one of many factors that complicates the question of mercury:

- There is no completely decisive test to find out how much mercury is stored in your body. Mercury levels in hair are a somewhat reliable indicator. A urine sample after taking dimercaptosuccinic acid (DMSA), a chelating drug, is another test that will be discussed below. (Chelating medicines— named from the Greek word for a "claw"—grab, or bind, heavy metals to neutralize and remove them.)

- There is no decisive test to determine your individual toler- ance to mercury or what problems any particular dose may cause after exposure at any given moment in your develop- ment or in combination with other toxins. There are, however, no tests of mercury toxicity that give us an idea of the dangers of low-level exposure. Richard Deth, Ph.D., has shown paralysis of one of chemistry's most important steps[*] by levels of Thimerosal that are one hundred times lower than what can be measured in babies a couple of weeks following a single Thimerosal-containing immunization.[1]

- The chelating medicines that pull mercury from your body or support your body's chemistry for detoxifying mercury may produce beneficial effects independent of any role they may have in removing mercury.

- One of the most puzzling factors is a rinsing paradox. When I wash my socks, most of the soap and dirt comes out with the first rinse. Each subsequent rinse produces less dirt until the socks come out clean. Never in washing my socks has the dirt stayed in them until the fourth rinse and then suddenly come pouring out. But something like this appears to happen in some people when they take repeated pulses of DMSA after failing to release much mercury into their urine after the first, second, or third three-day course of treatment.

- Symptoms of mercury toxicity fall within the realm of every medical specialty (pediatrics, internal medicine, family prac- tice, dermatology, neurology, gynecology, etc.). But most regular specialists visited by patients for possible mercury- related symptoms are not usually aware of mercury as a potential factor.

- Many practicing physicians remember giving mercury- containing medications with the understanding that the tox- icity of such medication was tolerable. This indifference to

---

[*]The re-methylation of homocysteine (see page 143).

the possible negative effects of mercury goes to some amazing extremes, including the use of mercury-containing thermometers, which if spilled could contaminate a household with what nowadays are considered dangerous amounts of mercury vapor.

- Drug companies and the FDA have permitted the use of mercury-containing preservatives in eyedrops as well as in immunizations injected into babies. The American Dental Association advocates the use of mercury-containing fillings, insisting on their safety and actively persecuting dentists who point out the dangers. These pro-mercury forces, combined with the medical profession's long history of using mercury as a medicine, slow down the spread of information that would lead most of us to avoid mercury until scientific methods are developed to determine individual tolerances for it.

- Fish is a significant source of mercury exposure. Mercury in seawater is passed up the food chain to the big fish, such as tuna. The microorganisms that take mercury from the water and pass it on to the tiny fish that eat them are also the originators of the good oils that are so important to correcting the lack of omega-3 fatty acids in our diets. Eat less fish and you get less good oil, but you are spared the burden of mercury. I resolve this dilemma by limiting my intake of fish, avoiding tuna and other large fish, and by taking my fish oil as a supplement, after making sure that the supplement is free of mercury, dioxins, and PCBs (polychlorinated biphenyls).

- Mercury's toxicity varies considerably among its different forms, with metallic mercury (quicksilver) causing little absorption when touched or swallowed, while mercury vapor and organic forms of mercury (methylmercury found in fish; ethylmercury found in Thimerosal, used as a preservative in vaccines and eyedrops) are nearly completely absorbed.

Mercury raises some tough questions, especially for those involved in the formation of public policy. It is one thing to protect the public from some new danger by requiring extensive studies of safety and effectiveness. It is another thing altogether to abolish practices that have been assumed, without carefully conducted studies, to be safe, but for which there is mounting evidence of danger. The difficulty of changing public policy is magnified when it involves the utterance of that forbidden medical word: "oops." Even when health professionals may be prepared to base new public policy on changing assessments of the risks of, say, dental amalgam, their lawyers may point to exposure to liability suits based on questions about what they knew and when they knew it, and further delay action.

Still, you don't have to make public policy; you have only to decide what is right for yourself and your family. Here are some steps I think you should consider. These steps are subject to revision! My own thinking about mercury has changed slowly over the last twenty years as I became more attentive to the work of colleagues, the experience of my patients, and the evolving scientific literature.[2]

1. Get your silver-mercury amalgam dental fillings replaced. Using the word *amalgam* for a Web search will bring you a list of sites providing both sides of this highly polarized debate on the dangers of mercury-containing fillings. At www.amalgam.org you will find information provided by DAMS (Dental Amalgam Mercury Syndrome) Inc., along with Consumers for Dental Choice, A Project of the National Institute for Science, Law and Public Policy, 1424 16th Street, NW, Suite 105, Washington, DC 20036. Included are protocols for dentists for safe amalgam removal provided by the International Academy of Oral Medicine and Toxicology (IAOMT).

2. Stop eating fish that contain high levels of mercury. Seafood contains more mercury than any other food. There is naturally occurring mercury in the oceans, but this is a tiny fraction compared to what has been added by human contamination. When people dispose of mercury, it finds its way to the sea. One study of dietary mercury intake gave a daily average of 1.3 mcg for the general population of the United States and 3.1 mcg for people living in New Jersey who ate fish. The range of intake was up to about seven times the average in people who ate more fish. Mercury levels in

various seafood products may vary considerably depending on their source location. Dr. Jon Pangborn conducted an informal study and found oysters, clams, and mussels were highest. Scallops and shrimp were high but are quite variable depending on the location. Shark and tuna were high (but tuna packed in water had little compared with tuna packed in oil). Seaweed can be the worst depending on location. Seaweed foods in a Japanese restaurant can be OK, but seaweed from Tampa Bay was ten to twenty times higher in mercury content than were the oysters off Sanibel Island. As a general rule, fish large enough to provide steaks come from predators at the top of the food chain where mercury becomes concentrated in the flesh of fish that have eaten the medium-size fish that have eaten the little fish that have eaten the tiny fish and vegetation. The smaller the fish, the lower the mercury content.

3. Once your teeth are mercury-free, have a urine test to see how much mercury comes out in your urine on the third day of taking a substance (DMSA, also called succimer; a pharmaceutical brand is Chemet) that draws mercury from your tissues into your urine. Such a test can be obtained from Great Smokies Diagnostic Laboratory (63 Zillicoa Street, Asheville, NC 28801-1074; Phone 800-522-4762) or Doctor's Data Laboratory (170 W. Roosevelt Road, West Chicago, IL 60185; Phone 800-323-2784; 708-231-3649). Both labs can provide you and your health-care provider with the details needed to carry out and interpret the test.

4. Depending on how you feel during and after your three-day dose of DMSA, and on the results of your urine test, consider taking DMSA along with a variety of supplements until either your urine levels fall to a minimum or you have a substantial improvement in symptoms.

Here is a regimen you and your physician can follow for taking DMSA and the supplements. It is adapted from the regimen for mercury detoxification or oxidative therapy from the DAN! (Defeat Autism Now!) Mercury Detoxification Consensus Group Position Paper (May 2001, James Laidler,

M.D., editor, Autism Research Institute, 4182 Adams Ave., San Diego, CA 92116; Phone: 619-281-7165; Fax: 619-563-6840).

- Set up a calendar so that you are on a two-week rotation, with three days on DMSA and eleven days off. Take all of the supplements every day, but you only take the succimer on days one through three of each cycle. Measure urinary toxic elements on the third day of succimer every two or three cycles. Depending on how things go, you should plan to complete at least six cycles. A blood count, including platelet count, and liver profile, BUN, and creatinine should be obtained every three to four weeks to monitor the potential toxicity of the DMSA.

- It is OK to interrupt the cycles for any reason. You may continue the supplements without the succimer, or just drop the whole thing in case of illness, travel, or other conflicts. The doses in the table below are geared to a child weighing forty pounds. If you weigh eighty pounds, you can double them; if you weigh 120, you can triple them; and so on.

Nutrient	Details	Dose	Per day
DMSA	Succimer, Chemet	200 mg	Three times
Vitamin C	Buffered ascorbic acid powder, 1 tsp = 4,400 mg	200 mg	Twice
Alpha lipoic acid	Thioctic acid	100 mg	Three times
Zinc	Picolinate or citrate	10 mg	Once (not with food)
Selenium	Oceanic	50 mg	Once
Vitamin E		100 mg	Once
Vitamin B_6	As pyridoxal 5 phosphate	25 mg	Once (in the morning)
Melatonin		1 mg	Once (at bedtime)
Taurine		200 mg	Once
Reduced glutathione		75 mg	Three times

In the past year I have started using a skin cream containing a form of vitamin B_1 with another cream containing reduced glutathione. This combination may provide a safer means for detoxification of mercury. Clinical experience and research has not ripened to the point of going into details, which can be obtained at www.autism.com/ari/dan/mercurydetox.html.

Lead

Like mercury, lead is heavy. To be technically correct, we'd have to call it dense, which means that a given volume weighs more than a given volume of other substances. A liter of lead weighs 11.3 kg. Recall that mercury is 13 kg per liter, so lead would float on mercury.

Lead and mercury are poisonous for some similar reasons. Their differences make assessment and treatment of lead poisoning a little less confusing than mercury. For one thing, there is no government agency, professional society, or industrial group insisting that lead be consumed in medications, dental fillings, or children's vaccines. Ever since leaded gasoline was discontinued some years ago, there has been broad agreement that zero is the right amount of lead to have in the environment as well as in our bodies. From the time of my training in pediatrics, when we regularly saw children from New Haven who had seizures and other dire symptoms after chewing on paint chips from old lead-painted houses, there has been ongoing discussion among professionals caring for children about what levels of lead are permissible and what levels should lead to varying intensity of treatment. While severe lead poisoning remains a problem, there is a growing body of research data supporting the concern that low levels of lead cause problems of attention, learning, and behavior in substantial numbers of our children. Public health and environmental policy may need further adjustments to lower our collective exposure. Still, as is the case with mercury, understanding how lead poisons you may impel you to make private health decisions long before public health authorities recommend such measures, if in fact they ever do.

Lead and mercury seem about as unsticky as substances can be. Sticky, however, they are: their atoms glom on to molecules in your body and steal their electrons (see Chapter 9), a process called oxidation, which can seriously impair their function. Because they are the heaviest, lead and mercury are among the worst of a long list of oxidative stresses that we encounter in our lives. Heavy atoms are set up to have a stronger pull of electrons—analogous to the stronger gravitational pull of larger planets.* That pull is the basis for the beneficial role of biologically tame metals, such as copper and zinc, which contribute their pull to enzymes and other large molecules where some serious electron pull is needed. Lead and mercury are too big to be tamed and their extra pull makes them difficult to get rid of, hence the need for the stickiness of detoxifying substances, such as reduced glutathione, explained elsewhere in this book.

The similarity between mercury and lead tends to end with their heaviness. Lead becomes deposited in bone because it resembles calcium. Lead is absorbed more readily in children with low calcium intake because lead is taken in as a calcium substitute. There is no such reservoir for mercury, which tends to be deposited more widely in the body and interferes with a greater variety of chemical functions.

The tests used to determine whether you have an excess body burden of mercury will also reveal lead. Hair analysis (which requires a bundle of the first inch of hair from the scalp about the diameter of a woman's finger), blood levels, urine levels, and especially urine levels following DMSA provocation each have their uses, depending on the form, route, and timing of the exposure that brought lead into your system. Lead testing is more reliable than mercury testing because of the narrower differences in the way lead affects different individuals as compared with mercury. If you have tests for lead poisoning, the tests will show a body burden that is likely to be below what current medical practice considers poisonous. For most of us and our children, our lead and mercury questions have to do with chronic, low-level exposure with measurements in a range well below the criteria for lead poisoning. As the debate continues over the lowest acceptable levels of lead in children, you can assume that those levels will continue to be set lower. The same will be true for adults, for whom measures to lower lead burdens will become more a part of medical practice.

---

*This is an oversimplification of the chemistry, but it's enough for you to understand the point.

Lead is more predicable than mercury in terms of the balance between body burden and a spectrum of negative effects that range from seizures, headache, abdominal pain, and irritability to problems of learning and behavior. Its removal from the body can be accomplished with less complex natural supplementation than I have described for mercury. Supplements of vitamin C, B_6 (as pyridoxal 5 phosphate), and calcium have been shown to be effective in lowering lead levels, even in industrial exposures. Taking 2,000 mg of vitamin C, 50 mg of pyridoxal 5 phosphate, and 1,500 mg of calcium as calcium citrate is a very low-risk strategy for an adult with evidence of an excess body burden of lead who wishes to avoid any risk associated with taking DMSA. DMSA is approved for treatment of lead poisoning. It works for mercury detoxification, but it is not yet approved by the U.S. Food and Drug Administration.

The regimen for mercury described on page 112 would also be effective as a chelating treatment for lead with the addition of a calcium supplement at the 1,500-mg dose. (Children need more calcium because they are growing; adults need more because they are big, so it's about the same dose for everyone.)

No one knows what price we are paying for the low level of lead exposure we all endure. As with mercury, there is no way to determine who is especially affected by small accumulations of lead. It took the human race hundreds of years to find out that the use of lead pipes for water, lead-containing materials for food containers, the ancient use of sweet-tasting lead acetate for covering the sour taste of turned wine, and the more recent use of lead acetate in paint could lead to disastrous health consequences. You are safer from the standpoint of lead toxicity than you are from mercury, because of the modern recognition of the hazards of lead. You will be even safer if you are aware that the recognition of the dangers of lead paint, lead-containing ceramic glazes, and lead-containing gasoline is something that has occurred during my lifetime. There are houses and dishes around that are much older than I am. Anyone with a chronic health problem should have his or her lead level checked and consider taking measures to reduce the level as much as possible. In addition, those of us who are healthy have significant ongoing risk of mercury exposure through dental fillings, seafood, and Thimerosal-containing vaccines. Prudence dictates having your body burden of mercury checked, which will let you know your lead status as well.

Aluminum

Like lead and mercury, aluminum is found in very low levels in our natural environment. It is not heavy but light, which is one reason it is one of the main components of the earth's outer and lighter crust as compared with the more dense deeper parts of the planet. Aluminum is part of many of the rocks you see everywhere you go. Unlike lead and mercury, it was not extracted as a metal from its ore for wide use until recently, when electric power was used for its refinement. Its utility in baking powder, antacids, antiperspirants, pots and pans (from which acid foods deliver significant amounts during cooking), foil, and, more controversially, as an ingredient in immunizations, raises the question of whether its special kind of stickiness should lead us to take strenuous steps to avoid it. The averages for one person have been reported[3] as follows (in milligrams):

Intake

In food and fluids	45.0
From airborne dust	0.1

Excretion

In feces	43.0
In urine	0.1
In sweat	1.0
In hair	0.0006
Unaccounted for	1.0

Aluminum is biochemically attracted to stick to the phosphates that form an active part of our DNA—the molecules that encode our ancestral memory and give us the instructions for making and replacing all the molecules in our body. The key to understanding why aluminum may be a particularly treacherous toxin is that it binds tightly. Even though lead and mercury are heavy and sticky, they do go through a process of turnover, in which appropriately sticky chelators, such as DMSA, can grab them in midair and send them off for detoxification. Not so with aluminum. Once it sticks to DNA it is there until the death of the cell carrying the DNA. Concern for the health of your permanent cells may make you mindful of staying away from aluminum.

Hair analysis and blood and urine levels give an idea of your body burden. They are variable from one day to the next, so I do not assume from one test that a patient has excess aluminum. Clues to aluminum toxicity can be obtained from urine organic acid levels. Alpha ketoglutarate levels may be low as a reflection of aluminum's toxicity. Since low manganese levels can do the same, you would need measurements of high aluminum to confirm the meaning of low urinary levels of alpha ketoglutarate.

There is no proven method for detoxifying aluminum and ridding it from your body. But you can avoid aluminum-containing pots and pans, keep foil out of direct contact with foods, and avoid aluminum-containing antiperspirants, antacids, and baking powder. You may not be able to do without immunizations for yourself or your children. Here is the dose of aluminum in various common U.S. immunizations, along with their manufacturers:

Vaccine	Manufacturer	Mg aluminum*
DTAP Infanrix	SmithKline Beecham	3.1
DTAP Certiv	North American Vaccine	2.5
DTAP Acel-Immune	Lederle	1.2
DTAP Tripedia	Pasteur Mérieux Connaught	0.9
DTP	Bioport	2.0
DTP	Connaught	0.5
DTP-HiB tetraimmune	Lederle	3.4
HepBHiB Comvam	Merck	0.7
HepB-Recombivax B	Merck	0.7
HepB-Engerix B	SmithKline Beecham	0.8
Tetanus	Lederle	2.9
Tetanus	Wyeth	5.1
Tetanus	SSVI	5.1

*Total in one immunizing series.
Source: FDA

Antimony, arsenic, beryllium, bismuth, cadmium, platinum, thallium, thorium, uranium, nickel, silver, tin, and titanium are other elements that appear in human tissues. Each has its own toxicity and it is beyond the scope of this book to describe them in detail. I chose mercury, lead, and aluminum for discussion because their toxicity is common. They have very different ways of poisoning us, and they present different problems in detoxification. As with all other potentially toxic elements, our exposure to them has occurred during a relatively short period in human history during which initial assumptions concerning their safety have been replaced by gradual recognition of the dangers they present. Dentists use approximately 300 metric tons of mercury annually for amalgam. It will ease your confusion in any debate over the relative safety of any toxin if you keep your focus on private health policy while others debate the health and economic trade-offs of public policy. Public health policy is aimed at statistically average people. Whoever you may be, you are not a statistical average.

7

Molecular Masquerade

Gluten and Cascin

JASON WAS A scrawny three-year-old boy. Pale, sad-faced, with dark circles under his eyes, he had never had a normal bowel movement. Yet he had never been quite sick enough for his pediatrician to offer more than reassurance that he would grow out of his listlessness, disturbed sleep, and irritability. At his mother's insistence, he was referred to the pediatric gastroenterologist at a university hospital and evaluated for an intestinal disorder. A biopsy of his small intestine revealed a loss of nap on the double velvet of the intestinal lining. This flattening of the villi, or complex microscopic absorptive projections of the bowel surface, is characteristic of celiac disease, a long-recognized consequence of intolerance to gluten. (Gluten is a protein found in cereal grains, such as wheat, rye, and barley.) Because Jason's blood tests for gluten sensitivity were normal, the specialist said that he did not meet all the criteria for celiac disease. His mother was told that he did not have gluten intolerance and no change in diet was advised.

When he first came to see me a couple of weeks later, I diagnosed him as the victim of an unreasonable dependence on laboratory results and research criteria. A person's body is quite often the best laboratory. As much as doctors and patients want objective evidence on which to base treatment—and as much as we want our patients to fit into standard research definitions of disease—sometimes we can do no better than a diagnostic trial of a treatment. I suggested that Jason embark on a brief trial of gluten avoidance. Within days he was better, and within weeks he was a new boy. He became energetic; gained weight and color in his cheeks; and had normal poops, sound sleep, and a calm disposition.

Alex was a seven-year-old autistic child who took pebbles from my driveway and made scratches on a mirror in my office. His speech was limited to chanting the last few words that were said to him, or to scripts from his videos. He made no eye contact. He was in constant motion, dashing, pacing, gesturing, grimacing, mouthing, sniffing, and intermittently bursting out in silly laughter. He had moments when he showed his detailed memory of long-past events and a verbatim recall of conversations, movies, or advertisements. His apparently good brain seemed poisoned with something like a psychedelic drug.

Much later, sitting and talking with Alex in my waiting room, I tried to detect traces of the autism he'd had when I first began treating him. Had I not met him before, there is no way I would have known that he had ever been in such trouble. The difference was his response to a gluten-free diet.

When such dramatic changes occur, you can perhaps understand why witnesses to the change become zealous evangelists. More than half of the autistic children I have known have improved enough on a gluten-free diet to make it worth continuing. The diet avoids wheat, rye, barley, and all products containing even traces of the protein (gluten) found in these grains but not in rice, corn, or millet. (Oats are still a matter of controversy; some studies show no negative effect in gluten-sensitive individuals, but other individuals report reactions to them.)

The majority of psychologists, physicians, teachers, neighbors, and parents reject the idea that anything as completely innocent as bread or spaghetti could make you lose your mind. It does not seem reasonable. Nor does depriving a child of food seem appropriate when he already has problems that limit his full enjoyment of life. Most people who consult me know that I will probably suggest changes in diet, supplements, or other aspects of their lives as part of the detective work to get to the bottom of chronic problems. Still, gluten avoidance is often a hard sell. If parents, grandparents, baby-sitters, teachers, and therapists (who often use food as a reward for good behavior or performance) are not supportive, implementing the needed changes can be impossible. Efforts to get everyone on board can bring charges of unfit parenting, and even child abuse, especially when divorce puts parents in opposition and the sympathies of the court can be recruited by an expert who testifies that "there is not a shred of credible evidence" that diet can cure autism. The key word here is "credible," and it simply means that the speaker does not believe whatever evidence he or she has examined, which is never all the existing evidence.

The abundant existing evidence divides into two sides that are so polarized that participants in the debate cannot hear each other at all. In my experience, the ultimate result of such conversations is frustration, anger, shouting, and then silence. Here is how things typically go: One party to the conversation, Joe, thinks of autism as a disease that develops in early childhood that affects communication, behavior, and socialization. Its cause is unknown and authoritative references point to no known treatment. End of story. Gluten sensitivity is not connected to its definition in the way that, say, the presence of strep germs is connected to the diagnosis of a strep throat. And gluten avoidance has nothing to do with the treatment of autism in the way that penicillin can be used to treat a strep throat. Joe usually points out that no double-blind randomized placebo-controlled studies have given statistical credibility to the benefits of a gluten-free diet in the treatment of autism. Thus, parents or practitioners who pursue such diets are without the protection offered by scientific consensus.

The other party to the conversation, Linda, thinks of the question in terms of the individual who carries a label representing her membership in a group of children who share certain problems of communication, behavior, and socialization. The child, not the disease, is the focus. The focal issue is whether that particular child may or may not respond to a gluten-free diet, considering that there are credible reports of others having done so. Such reports, credible as they may be, are anecdotal and lack the standing of group statistics.

Joe is talking about treating a disease and Linda is talking about treating the individual. Joe is talking about public health policy; Linda about private health policy. Joe is talking about a scientific model for establishing proof that is necessary and suited to drug trials and can be paid for with the kinds of profits made from an effective new drug. Linda is talking about a scientific model suited to physics and astronomy where a single good observation can prove a theory.

In my experience, most scientifically trained practitioners start out like Joe and end up more like Linda. When it comes to gluten, a single experience with a patient or family member is usually enough to push us over the line. I started out as a Joe. It was years after learning about the convincing studies of Dohan and Dohan from the 1950s and 1960s that my prescription of a gluten-free diet for individuals with schizophrenia and autism changed from being a last resort to being near the top of the treatment list. Like many who have not traveled this road, I was waiting for more proof to impress the Joe in me. In the end, it was seeing children respond the way Alex did that made me a believer. What do I believe? I believe that you may be missing the boat if you have any chronic symptom and you have not tried eliminating gluten from your diet for somewhere between three weeks and three months to see what difference it may make.

Look at the following list. Is it any wonder that a medical mind, like Joe's, conditioned to think that each disease has a separate cause, and each cause produces a separate disease, has difficulty believing that sensitivity to the protein in wheat, rye, barley, and, maybe, oats could produce such a diverse list of conditions?

- Headache
- Fatigue
- Malaise
- Depression
- Any sort of chronic digestive problem including difficulty gaining weight, abdominal pain, diarrhea, constipation, irritable bowel, undigested food in stools
- Sjögren's syndrome (dry eyes)
- Epilepsy associated with brain calcification, history of migraine headaches, hyperactivity, or digestive problems
- Osteoporosis
- Infertility, complications of pregnancy such as miscarriage, low-birth-weight infants
- Intestinal lymphoma
- Esophageal cancer

- Diabetes
- Thyroid problems
- Schizophrenia
- Autism
- Dermatitis herpetiformis (a chronic skin condition with tiny blisters that resemble those of herpes virus infections)

There is substantial evidence of a causative association between gluten intolerance and these problems. And the list grows as case reports of dramatic cures produced by a gluten-free diet attract the attention of researchers. The research model demands finding groups of similar people (that is, with the same diagnosis) who can be used to make a statistical case regarding the role of gluten in that disease.

You, however, are not a group. You are an individual. Regardless of whether your symptoms put you into a diagnostic group and provide you with a label for your problems, you still need to make personal decisions about your health, looking for safe, inexpensive, and relatively easy steps that may get you out of trouble. You do not need to wait for a group to belong to; all you need to do is test yourself for gluten sensitivity. There are blood tests and urine tests that predict fairly reliably whether you will feel better by eliminating gluten from your diet. But no blood or urine test is completely decisive. Response to a change in diet will be decisive for you. Medical research demands standard definitions for judging the effectiveness of a particular treatment. It would not do for one researcher to claim success based on treating people who defined their gluten sensitivity in terms of feeling better on a diet, while another used a strict definition based on changes in the lining of the gut as determined by biopsy. But you, Linda, and I do not have to worry about the disease definitions necessary for comparability of research studies. We only have to worry about safety, cost, and efficacy. Then, if something works, we can wonder about *how* it works and whether there might be some way around a permanent and strict avoidance of gluten.

How Does Gluten Sensitivity Work?

Wheat is one of the seven grains. The others are rice, barley, oats, corn, millet, and rye. Each is a modern hybrid of wild grasses that were domesticated with the beginning of agriculture twelve to fifteen thousand years ago. The grass seeds contain starch energy stored against the day when the seeds find soil in which to germinate new plants. The starch is enclosed in a coat of fiber and protein, which makes up less than 10 percent of the resulting flour when the seeds are crushed and ground in a mill.

The grasses that were the ancestors of modern wheat had a few arrow-shaped kernels, which our ancestors could gather from the stems or from the ground in the times before women noticed and then organized the conditions for their germination and cultivation. Over a period of a few thousand years, the early farmers favored the wild grasses that produced nice fat seeds and learned how to select and then hybridize for size, taste, resistance to drought, and consistency.

Consistency became a big issue after the development of fermentation gave rise to barm, the yeasty sediment formed during the production of wine and beer. Yeast-rich barm, kneaded into moist wheat flour, formed little bubbles in the dough to create raised bread. The stickier the dough, the better the bubbles. Gluten is gluey; it was the central ingredient in the paste we used to use (and sometimes eat) in kindergarten. The same glueyness gives wheat the stickiness needed to make pasta as well as to form the bubbles in leavened bread.

During Roman times one kind of wheat (siligo) was used for bread making, and spelt, with lower gluten content, was used for soups. Both had kernels that stayed on the stem until harvest. By that time, the farming peoples of the Middle East had invaded and substantially replaced the original peoples of Northern Europe, who, like the peoples of the Americas, Africa, and the Far East, had not adapted to the consumption of wheat because they were hunter-gatherers or because they practiced agriculture based on corn (maize), millet (sorghum), or rice, as well as tubers.

Nowadays, the descendants of the original population of Europe remain relatively poorly adapted to gluten, so a population of largely European origins has an incidence of gluten intolerance of about one out of every hundred people. Populations of African, Asian, or Native American descent also have a high incidence of gluten intolerance. Researchers know about this incidence largely through studies of the intestinal lining of family members of individuals with gluten-induced malabsorption (celiac disease). Many of these individuals are not (yet) sick, although their intestinal velvet manifests changes, which, were they visible on the skin, would be clearly unhealthy. The picture of gluten intolerance has changed over the past century from scrawny pot-bellied infants and children dying of wasting and diarrhea to the wide spectrum of illnesses I listed earlier.

It is a mystery why food intolerance could devastate whole regions of the intestine. Even more mysterious is the mechanism by which gluten mischief reaches the brain, skin, and other organs remote from the gut. (Keep in mind, by the way, that nothing is really very remote from anything else in the body, least of all the brain and the gut, whose relationship is eloquently portrayed in the book *The Second Brain* by Michael Gershon.)

One solution to the mystery begins with the digestion of protein. A protein is an assembly of amino acids. Imagine about twenty different shapes and colors of paper clips. Put on some good music, sit down on the floor, and start assembling the paper clips into a chain. If each paper clip were an amino acid, then the first two you join together would be called a di-peptide (di = two). Add one more and it would be a tri-peptide. After that, they are just called peptides until you have about 100 or so. Then it becomes a small protein. Most proteins have hundreds or thousands of amino acids, and they are folded into shapes that are kept permanent by sticky bridges, usually made of sulfur. When you get a perm at the hair salon they put stuff on your hair to break the sulfur bridges, then set your hair before putting on some other stuff to re-form the sulfur bridges. The strength of hair (try breaking a plait of just twenty strands of hair with your bare hands) is enormous, so imagine the problem your digestive tract has when you are obliged to disassemble the thousands of amino acids from your food right down to individual paper clips, which then pass into your bloodstream to be reassembled into your very own proteins. A combination of a bath in acid (in your stomach), followed by a bath in alkali (in your small intestine), combined with the frantic work of large proteins (digestive enzymes) embracing your food proteins and unhooking the paper clips at a dizzying pace, does the job.

The job is done more efficiently because one group of enzymes breaks the paper-clip chain into chunks (peptides) and another nibbles amino acids from the ends of the chunks. The chunk-makers are proteases and the chunk-nibblers are peptidases. Gluten intolerance has to do with a failure of a particular peptidase called DPP4. (When the same enzyme is sticking out of a lymphocyte and apparently doing a different job within the body, it is also called CD26.) Because of the failure or insufficiency of DPP4, an undigested fragment of protein, or peptide, survives. It appears to cause mischief in at least two ways.

First, this undigested peptide, which is eight amino acids still joined together, looks familiar to the immune system. It is another instance of mimicry. In this case, the wheat protein did not mean to produce a fragment that might fake out the immune system of the person consuming and poorly digesting the protein. (Other instances of mimicry in nature and medicine are quite intentional, such as the molecules produced by fungi that mimic and block our energy-producing chemistry.) In the case of gluten-derived peptides, the mimicry is purely coincidental. It is based on digestive weakness among the descendants of peoples who have not been eating wheat long enough to adapt, or whose digestive difficulty goes along with some other trait that has a survival benefit. Either way, many people have such a problem with digestion and some of them have or will have symptoms caused by the triggering of an immune response against the suspicious-looking peptide.

What does the peptide look (or taste, or feel, or sound) like to the cells of the immune system that are constantly on border patrol? Probably a virus. Because the gluten-derived peptide is similar to various disease-causing viruses, it generates a complex defensive response on the part of the immune system, which does not then find a virus to kill. The next step in the chain of events is damage to tissues by the antibodies aimed at the peptide. This triangle of viral stimulus, immune response, and autoimmune damage is suspected to be a common theme in various illnesses, such as type I diabetes, multiple sclerosis, and autism. In summary, the first way that undigested peptides from gluten cause trouble is by stimulating an autoimmune response that damages different tissues in different people.

The second way that undigested peptides from gluten cause trouble is by entering the bloodstream, which some peptides tend to do in the normal course of things. The vast majority of protein-derived amino acids enter the bloodstream only after being digested down to individual amino acids. In this case, though, in individuals whose intestinal lining is leaky—in the sense that unwanted molecules leak from the intestine into the bloodstream—an excess of undigested peptides enters the bloodstream.

Peptides released from gluten when there is a failure of DPP4 possess another kind of mimicry apart from their resemblance to peptides from viruses. These peptides look like opium. So, when the DPP4 enzyme fails to do its job in the digestion of gluten, the peptides released mimic not only viruses, but also opium and the family of drugs derived from opium: heroin, morphine, codeine, and other semisynthetic derivatives that are unequaled in alleviating pain. The way this family of molecules relieves pain is based on their mimicry of endorphins, natural substances our bodies release when we are under the stress of exertion or injury. Opioid is the name of the whole family of substances that act like opium-derived drugs and endorphins.

Our current understanding of this second mechanism for mischief caused by gluten is based on the finding of opioid peptides in the urine of individuals with autism and schizophrenia. Another body of evidence comes from the experience of people such as Alex, whose improvement following gluten avoidance is dramatic and not explained by any other treatment. Of the hundreds of autistic children I've treated in my practice, more than half have stuck with a gluten-free diet after (reluctantly) trying it. A third body of evidence comes from observing the dramatic withdrawal symptoms that occur in some individuals when they come off gluten. The malaise and irritability strongly resemble a mild version of the kinds of symptoms seen in heroin withdrawal.

A Trial of Gluten Avoidance

If you think that any of your symptoms may be related to sensitivity to gluten, the first rule is to embark on a gluten-free diet gradually. Unless you do all your own cooking from scratch, it is not easy to avoid gluten. For your child, unless you are the sole source of her food, you will have to recruit the understanding and active cooperation of anyone who might give her food: other kids' parents, her school, and siblings and relatives. When a child has problems, depriving her of food she likes seems, at best, odd and, at worst, abusive, to lots of well-meaning people, including some who may carry a lot of weight in your family (such as grandparents). Here are the steps you should take:

1. Let everyone know that you plan to start a gluten-free diet as of a certain date. Make it clear that the diet is for medical diagnostic purposes and will last initially for three weeks, with the proviso that it could be extended to three months before making a decision about the long term.

2. Have them read this chapter or another reference for some background.

3. If they are not willing to provide only gluten-free food, have them agree to provide no food at all, allowing you to produce foods for your child for birthday parties, school events, lunches, and visits outside your home.

4. Equip yourself with a guide that provides the details necessary to carry out the diet, including sources of gluten-free food, recipes, hints, and other resources. The best one I know is *Special Diets for Special Kids* by Karen Seroussi and Lisa Lewis. This book is written for the parents of autistic kids, but the methods for carrying out the diet are the same, regardless of the symptoms for which a diet is needed. Also see www.autismndi.com and www.gfcfdiet.com.

If you want to try a gluten-free diet for yourself—and you're sure you can exist for three weeks while making all your own food—then the rules are simple enough. Be sure to exclude anything made with flour from wheat, rye, barley, or oats, and any other product that came originally from those sources. Most individuals with gluten-related symptoms will begin to experience relief a few days after excluding all gluten. It may take up to three weeks before you can definitively say whether or not avoiding gluten has produced the desired effect. At that point, if you have not experienced any improvement, you might want to put the gluten question on the back burner. You can return to a three-month exclusion of gluten as a more final test after considering other explanations for your symptoms. For instance, you may want to have some lab tests that could strengthen or weaken the case against gluten.

Lab Tests for Gluten Sensitivity

There is no lab test that will determine decisively whether you will respond to a gluten-free diet. However, there are lab tests, which, if abnormal, will predict a good response to a gluten-free diet. If their results are normal, these same tests may diminish your hopes for a notable response to dietary change. Many doctors define the problem in terms of the lab test, not in terms of your response to a change in diet. For the most part, the lab tests are meant to indicate celiac disease, which does not necessarily have a one-to-one correlation with all of the other problems associated with gluten sensitivity. Celiac disease is just one type of a broader spectrum of gluten sensitivity.

The following lab tests can be used to predict that a gluten-free diet will relieve symptoms that might be caused by gluten sensitivity. They are listed in order of increasing predictive value.

1. Urine test for intestinal permeability.* This test may point to gluten problems when an abnormally low absorption of mannitol is found.
2. Blood tests:
   * Antibodies to wheat, rye, oats, and barley. IgG antibodies may turn up in a screening test for food allergies, called an IgG ELISA, in which your blood is tested for reactivity to many foods. The more and the stronger your reaction to these foods, the more likely that other, more specific tests for gluten sensitivity will turn out to be positive.
   * Antibodies to tissue transglutaminase, endomysium, reticulin, and gliadin (a subfraction of gluten). Elevated levels of IgA antibodies to one or more of these substances correlate strongly with celiac disease. If any of these tests is positive, it is a strong indication that you should try a gluten-free diet to see if it clears your symptoms.
   * Small bowel biopsy. This is currently done by upper gastrointestinal endoscopy. A flexible tube is passed down your esophagus, past your stomach, and into your small

---

*Lactose-mannitol absorption test. Available from Great Smokies Diagnostic Laboratory.

intestine, where small snips (biopsies) can be collected for microscopic examination. If this test shows that you have a smoothing of the normally velvety nap of the lining of your small intestine, then you should change your diet and see if that corrects the abnormality.

Suppose that one or more of these tests are abnormal and you change your diet for as long as three months and still experience no change in the way you feel or function. Should you remain on a gluten-free diet indefinitely, hoping to prevent future mischief? This is a tough question that can be answered either way, depending on the circumstances. The problems I listed at the beginning of this chapter suggest that the stakes are quite high. On the other hand, a gluten-free diet is inconvenient. In general, I lean toward taking these lab tests seriously if they are abnormal.

None of the experts I have talked with believe that taking an enzyme that will do the job of DPP4 will eliminate the need for a gluten-free diet. Most, however, feel that such an enzyme—to be taken at the beginning of a gluten-containing meal—is helpful. It may not permit gluten-sensitive individuals to eat bread and pasta, but it should relieve them of vigilant concern over the hidden gluten content of prepared foods. It can be obtained from Kirkman Labs by visiting www.kirkmanlabs.com or by calling 800-245-8282.

Casein Sensitivity

Everything I have described regarding gluten applies to casein, one of the main proteins in milk (and the sticky protein familiar to you as Elmer's Glue). Just as there are people in the population who have not adapted to the consumption of certain cereal grains, there are others who are unable to digest milk. I have chosen to leave casein sensitivity out of the discussion until now to avoid confusion. The confusion comes from the different ways milk products can be toxic.

The first way has to do with the lack of a DPP4 peptidase enzyme that fails to cleave to a mischievous peptide within the casein molecule.

This problem is fully equivalent to the gluten problem I described above. On lab tests, antibodies to casein are a positive indicator, but not as reliable as the antibody tests used to identify gluten sensitivity. Small bowel biopsy is not relevant to the diagnosis of casein sensitivity because casein does not injure the bowel in that particular way. Another test is being developed that promises to be the best one for the peptide problems caused by gluten and/or casein. As I have described, the peptides pass into the blood, where they do harm because they evoke an autoimmune response and/or they mimic endorphins to cause changes in perception, mood, and behavior. Like everything in the blood, the peptides pass through the kidneys, so that some of them appear in the urine. For a number of years, researchers have been able to measure these peptides. However, the tests have not yet been perfected to the point where they can substitute for a change in diet. Casein sensitivity requires a shorter interval—three weeks—in order to judge whether an elimination diet effectively improves symptoms.

Milk allergy, the second way in which milk products can be a problem, does not have a clear-cut boundary with casein sensitivity. Milk allergy comes to about the same thing: it can produce just about any symptom you can think of. Allergy, in the usual sense of the word, has the medical implication of an immune system reaction that differs from the peptide issue I have just described. With allergy, the protein in milk (usually casein) causes either an immediate allergic reaction in the form of hives, eczema, swelling, itching, or digestive complaints, or a delayed reaction that can take almost any form. The delayed reaction is much more difficult to track to its origin because the symptoms may occur at varying intervals and intensities after eating different milk products.

The third milk-related problem is lactose intolerance. Lactose is the sugar found in the milk from any mammal. Just as there are people descended from ancestors without a long history of consuming gluten, there are many without a long history of consuming nonhuman milks. Among such peoples are individuals who cannot digest lactose, a molecule made up of two simple sugars: glucose and galactose. They lack the enzyme needed to separate these sugars so that each can be absorbed into the bloodstream. As a consequence, the undigested lactose travels down the digestive tract where the normal germ population consumes it. The result is bowel urgency, cramps, diarrhea, and gas, within an hour after eating lactose-containing food. A test (hydrogen breath tests) can distinguish lactose intolerance from other milk-related problems.

If you experience symptoms outside the digestive tract from milk products, then milk allergy or casein sensitivity is the problem. If your symptoms are purely digestive, then you can only distinguish between milk allergy and lactose intolerance by doing the hydrogen breath test. The value of knowing the difference is that there are commercially available lactose-free milk products. Also, you can add lactase to milk products to make up for your own lack of this enzyme. If, on the other hand, your problem is a milk allergy, you will need to avoid milk and all milk products.

8

DNA

I AM NOT sure when I first heard gonads referred to as "the family jewels." It was probably during recess in the fourth grade when contact sports increased the risk of gonadal injury at a time when my schoolmates and I experienced the dawning of interest in reproductive physiology. I understood the value of those jewels in terms of avoiding the pain that might come from a misdirected kick or elbow, or a fall onto a fence or the bar that distinguished my bike as a boys bike with its special peril for boys' gonads. I misunderstood a number of details concerning the reproductive value of the jewelry and, even when I got the basic facts straight, I still did not understand that I was the protector of the genetic material of a family that extended immeasurably behind me to my ancestors and might extend continuously beyond me to those whose ancestor I would someday be. I certainly did not understand that oxidative stress was a greater threat than the crossbar on my bicycle to my DNA (genes, chromosomes, genetic endowment).

DNA or deoxyribonucleic acid is inherently less susceptible to oxidation than the very unsaturated fatty acids of my cell membranes (see Chapter 10). The latter have electrons that are particularly susceptible to being grabbed by any other molecule, such as oxygen, that has a hunger for them. Fatty acids are crucial to the structure of cells and serve as raw material for making hormones, but DNA is the bearer of information from the past to the future. If the cell membrane becomes damaged, the cell's function may suffer. If DNA becomes damaged, the misinformation that results may engender more serious and lasting consequences: for you, if it is in any cell of your body; or for your off-spring, if it is in one of the few eggs or sperms that you will use to make a family. The integrity of your DNA is so important that you have a repair mechanism to fix DNA molecules in any cell of your body. The message of this chapter is "Maintain your DNA."

Meet SAM. SAM is a molecule with a long name, s-adenosylme-thionine, so we call it SAM for short. It is a relatively small molecule, a few times bigger than, say, one of the amino acid paper clips that are the subunits of protein, and you wouldn't even notice it next to a DNA molecule, which is made up of thousands of units, each of which is about SAM's size. SAM has an exclusive* franchise, a distributorship. SAM has cornered the market for delivering the most fundamental material needed for making and repairing molecules all over your bio-chemistry: single carbon atoms in the form we call methyl groups.

There is no molecule in your body that is not based on carbon atoms. Carbohydrate, fat, protein, hormones, neurotransmitters, and all of the other hundred thousand different kinds of molecules that make up your body are all based on the stringing together of carbon atoms, which in turn may connect with oxygens, hydrogens, nitrogens, sulfur, phosphorus, and so on. The fundamental structural unit, a car-bon atom, is so ubiquitous and so apparently available that it seems odd that there is a need for special arrangements to have it delivered to wherever it is needed for new construction or repair and it seems even more odd that there should be just one guy with the whole fran-chise. I would have thought that such special arrangements would be needed for nitrogen. It is needed for the synthesis of all sorts of impor-tant molecules—amino acids, proteins, and nucleic acids—and yet sin-gle nitrogens are moved easily from one molecule to another in a process of transamination. Indeed, the nitrogen we do obtain in our diet has to come more or less prepackaged in about a dozen essential amino acids that serve as raw materials for important molecules (neu-

---

*Molecules derived from the vitamin folic acid have a subcontract for delivery of single carbon groups for making nucleotides, the basis for DNA and RNA as well as for another key methylation step.

rotransmitters, proteins). SAM, in fact, is made from one of these essential amino acids: methionine. SAM will reenter my story after discovering a jewel thief at the shoe store.

I, the fourth grader, leave my boys bike in the driveway and join my mother for a trip to two of my favorite stores: May's department store with escalators to ride, and Roentgen's shoe store, where you can look right at the bones of your feet in the x-ray machine.

I was delighted by the device that let me stand on a platform and watch a screen above it display my wiggling toe bones in action surrounded by the staccato images of the shoe nails and topped by the circles of eyelets for my laces. X-rays streamed through my feet and crashed into the phosphor on the fluoroscope screen where the particles of light (photons) were exchanged for some that I could see and that varied with the density encountered by the rays as they traversed my foot. This was really neat. My toes in action. Seeing the invisible. My mother would not let me linger long on the machine. No one else was waiting to use it, but one needed to set boundaries on how much fun to extract from the situation that did not have the natural limit of an ice-cream cone. Propriety, not jeopardy, was the guideline. My mother did not conceive that there might be a danger to the family's DNA hanging in direct line of the x-rays.

The danger was that a high-energy photon would go crashing through my molecules and on the way it would knock off an electron, which would need to be replaced, perhaps from a fatty acid in a cell membrane. (The "oxidative damage" caused by the x-ray beam and the repairative role of antioxidants will be explained further in Chapter 10.) Then either the cell membrane would suffer damage or vitamin C and all the other antioxidants would rescue the situation. As the x-ray photons streamed through my various parts, every molecule in my body was at risk of losing an electron. The potential for damage depended not only on the local supply of antioxidants but on the kind of cell and kind of molecule that might take the hit. As I changed my socks to try on a pair of sneakers, a few superficial skin cells would have been loosened to provide lunch for the dust mites that inhabited the carpet of the shoe store. If the fatty acid membranes of these cells had just been damaged by the passing x-rays, I would go free of harm. If some injury occurred to most of the parts of most of the cells of my body, the consequences would dissipate with the death of that cell in due course as the cell finished its allotted time.

If, however, the photon from the machine collided with a DNA molecule and knocked off an electron, this oxidative damage to the information stores of my body would threaten me in one of three ways unless the damage were to be repaired. One way could distort the information package presented by a dividing cell in any part of me so that its daughter cell, the daughter's daughters, and so on, could perpetuate the distortion, altering the function of a whole line of cells. Certain kinds of distorted information could lead to a line of cells that gave up their allegiance to me and set up an independent, cancerous existence as the ultimate effect of the hit from the machine in the shoe store. A second way could distort the information package of one of the permanent undividing cells of my brain or immune system and so pollute or diminish the irreplaceable small reservoir of the cells that form the basis of the self I was and would become. A third way could distort the information package of the family jewels. An alteration in the DNA of a sperm-producing cell, if not repaired, could harm the information entrusted to me by my ancestors and steal that legacy from my offspring.

I seem to have survived my trip to the shoe store. I continue to sense the presence of that same little boy in me still, and no maverick cells have caused any more of a threat than a few precancerous clusters on my bald head, where some tropical sun did the kind of damage that the shoe store x-rays appear to have failed to do. My daughters seem to carry a full set of ancestral genes. My DNA has remained functional despite countless oxidative attacks on the electrons of its double-stranded molecules. But what if harm were to be done to my DNA? Enter SAM the repairman, with his supply of methyls to help replace broken parts in my DNA. Note that the broken part here is one that concerns information, not structure. The fatty acid velvet that makes up the basic fabric of the cellular membranes of my body is important as a component of these key structures. If membranes get damaged, the harm is limited to the cell in question and may be more or less important depending on whether the cell is a transient skin cell or a part of my permanent cells. In either case the damage is not multiplied. If the damaged cell were to be one that does multiply (that is, divide), the defect would, if anything, be diluted in the process.

DNA, however, is a molecule that contains information. If it is damaged, the harm will spread to future generations of the cell, which may be future generations of one's family if the cell is a sperm or an egg from which a child emerges. At the very least the damage will spread to the cells that arise from the afflicted cell unless the damage is repaired. An elaborate mechanism exists in the nucleus of each of your cells for the repair of DNA molecules that have been altered by oxidative damage. The crucial intermediary in that mechanism is folic acid, a B vitamin, which has a major role in preventing cancer by supporting the synthesis of healthy DNA and the repair of damaged DNA.[1] The reason that we are so preoccupied by the toxic effects of radiation—from x-ray machines to sunlight—is that the damage it causes to DNA may be passed from cell to cell. Otherwise, it would not be worth the body's effort to nullify the effects of damage to DNA. As it stands, the body's effort uses resources that come from the food we eat, and the food we eat is often not sufficient even if we eat very well. The dose of folic acid required to assist in the repair of damaged DNA is well beyond the current RDA.

The Importance of Folic Acid

Some people with a special need for folic acid end up having babies with birth defects, others end up with heart disease, and still others with lung, esophageal, bowel, or uterine cancers. Many people with any one of those problems got their problem from causes that have nothing to do with folic acid. Knowing the name and knowing the cause may be very different exercises.

If you came to me as a smoker, as a woman thinking about starting a pregnancy, as a person with a history of colitis, as a woman with a repeatedly abnormal Pap smear, or as a person with a blood test indicating a high level of homocysteine, I would include the same steps as part of my recommendation: large doses of folic acid regardless of your diagnosis. In each case the folic acid has the same job working as SAM's agent in distributing methyls to DNA chemistry. Methylation is such an important part of chemistry that it deserves a status along with helping your molecules hang on to their electrons. DNA is protected by antioxidant mechanisms, but its repair depends on an interconnected group of substances that have other additional important tasks worthy of your understanding. This group consists of amino acids* that are the sources of methyl groups, SAM, folic acid, vitamin B_{12}, and vitamin B_6.

Methionine is the queen of amino acids. There are twenty-two different amino acids in the royal family of nitrogen-bearing molecules, all but one of which** join together to form small aggregates of two to a dozen, known as peptides, or huge aggregates of thousands, known as proteins. An elite group of amino acids have assignments as individuals*** apart from contributing to the formation of peptides and proteins.

The queen of these few independent royal agents, Methionine, owes her monarchy to the special versatility of her triple endowment: 1) Methyls, single carbon units; 2) Sulfur, an element with important qualities of stickiness; and 3) Nitrogen, the defining ingredient of amino acids. Let us watch Methionine as she carries out her royal duties. She enters the courtroom carrying the methyl treasure. She receives a message that single carbon atoms are needed to repair the royal treasure house, where the genealogy and all the memories of the kingdom are preserved from generation to generation. She anticipates the (temporary) loss of her treasure and, unable to part with it and still maintain her identity, she dons a costume and becomes SAM, who, with the help of folic acid, repairs DNA. As SAM she is transformed in the process and becomes a mean, dangerous molecule that poses a great threat to the kingdom unless it is satisfied by being assigned to the kingdom's most valuable project (sanitation) or by being reendowed with a methyl to recover its status. The dangerous molecule in question is Methionine's dark alter ego, Horrible Homocysteine. This molecule is a prime example of how toxic one's own chemistry can become without any influence from tick bites, germs, rancid oils, or radiation. No matter what sort of toxic food you may eat, poisonous air you may

---

*Methionine, histadine, serine, and glycine.

**Taurine. It functions as a free agent and does not make up a part of larger molecules. It can be used if consumed as such, but under ordinary circumstances it is made from methionine.

***For example, tyrosine is used for forming thyroid hormone as well as norepinephrine. Tryptophan is the raw material needed for making another neurotransmitter, serotonin.

breathe, or contaminated water you may drink, you will have a hard time finding in your environment as mean a molecule as homocysteine. You have approximately one chance in fifty of being poisoned by your own homocysteine for the simple reason that you are not meeting your quirky needs for folic acid, vitamin B_6, or vitamin B_{12}. The first warnings[2] of homocysteine's harmful habits came from a Harvard Medical School faculty member, Kilmer S. McCully, whose 1960 propositions have finally been confirmed thirty years after his initial reports were rejected by his colleagues.

In the first year of medical school we students heard stories about medical giants of the past who were hounded or even hung for their dissent from current views. I thought that our professors meant that such practices had been discontinued and that science had become open to the rapid acceptance of sound ideas and the fair treatment of their proponents. McCully is one of many people of the present generation whose treatment by his peers illustrates that science is not the objective realm of dispassionate weighers and measurers that it is cracked up to be. Even if it were, it might take years for any new idea to catch on while enduring the heat of scientific skepticism and suffering the necessary delays of publication, discussion, and replication. The time it takes to get new ideas across is at least doubled by the workings of egos and personal conflicts that worm their way into any competitive activity.

When McCully fingered homocysteine he had a pretty good handle on how it might interact with oxidative stress to be the main cause of cardiovascular disease in many people. An up-to-date expansion and elaboration of his ideas by Stamler and Slivka[3] was brought to my attention by Jeffrey Bland who pointed out that this is one of the key articles in the current literature. It covers the interconnections of sulfur amino acid chemistry with many other activities in biochemistry. Here are the main points translated into the terms I have been using. If you understand them, you will be able to grasp a number of related advances in chemistry that will influence your health over the next few years.

1. Methionine and its alter ego, homocysteine, have a relationship that exemplifies other situations in biochemistry in which a particularly helpful and healthful molecule is just

one step away from being a particularly toxic one. The very
properties that give value to a molecule (such as the combined
close presence of sulfur-, nitrogen-, oxygen-, and carbon-
containing groups in methionine) can give rise to compounds
that may be versatile and useful on the one hand or quite
troublesome on the other.

2. As I will explain later, one of the chief ways our bodies quench
the potential toxicity of hormones such as excess estrogen, as
well as various neurotransmitters and all kinds of unwanted
foreign molecules, is to stick on a sulfur-oxygen group called
sulfate. In the case of the damage done by homocysteine, it
appears that the main harm done to blood vessels and other
tissues in the body is a misuse of sulfation so that healthy
tissues are, in a distorted sense of the word, detoxified. As I
mentioned previously and will describe more fully in Chapter
9, detoxification involves adding sticky stuff to stinky
molecules (such as sulfur) to render them more manageable. If
you start sticking sulfates where they co-opt the desired
adhesion between molecules in healthy tissue, then the tissue
becomes weakened, not only losing its structural integrity but
opening the way for oxidative stress to do its mischief. People
with a risk of cardiovascular disease will benefit from
understanding the relationship between the damage done by
homocysteine and the protection afforded by antioxidants.

3. The behavior of homocysteine actually liberates free radicals
to do their mischief, reminding us that the external environment is not the exclusive source of oxidative damage.
Consider what would happen if you, captivated by Queen
Methionine, decided to eat lots of protein or take supplements
of methionine so that you would have plenty of methyls to
maintain your DNA. If you happen to be a person with weak
mechanisms for transforming homocysteine to its job in the
sanitation department or back into methionine, you will
unleash homocysteine on your chemistry and do yourself
harm. About one third of individuals with cardiovascular
disease have a tendency to the damage produced by high
levels of homocysteine.[4] If you have a personal or family

history of vascular disease, it would be a factor (among others, including a need for extra magnesium, a need for more unsaturated fatty acids, and, of course, a tendency to high cholesterol levels) to weigh in assessing your situation.

Use the following test to measure your homocysteine level: eat meat, poultry, eggs, fish, or beans at every meal for twenty-four hours or take a methionine supplement, 250 mg four times in twenty-four hours, while you collect a twenty-four-hour urine specimen for measurement of homocysteine. Alternatively, you could have a blood specimen taken at the end of the period for homocysteine measurement. An abnormally high level calls for a trial of folic acid and, perhaps, vitamin B_6 and B_{12} and betaine (trimethylglycine) supplementation followed by repeated testing to confirm your success in removing homocysteine from your body. Once the test is done, you will need to understand that a high intake of protein, with its load of homocysteine, may be beneficial or harmful depending on how well you have taken care of your homocysteine problem with the vitamin supplements that suit your particular quirk.

Stamler and Slivka speculate that pacifying homocysteine in individuals with high levels may be also accomplished with various substances, including feverfew extract, which permit covering the sticky sulfur with a nitrogen-bearing group.

4. Next, if you are wondering why such a toxic transformation of methionine should exist at all, the answer is that homocysteine is needed to make methionine's most useful metabolite, reduced glutathione (RG). RG is the most important worker in the detoxification department, the resupplier of vitamin E (see Chapter 10). In fact, detoxification is the most important activity in the body's biochemistry. To remind you of one of the key points in this book: *getting rid of toxins that come in from the outside, whether they be lead, mercury, arsenic, or a variety of toxic chemicals; dumping used chemicals that are generated in our own chemistry; and detoxifying nasty substances that come from the germs*

that inhabit our intestines are the body's biggest consumers of energy for making new molecules. Reduced glutathione is a peptide made of three amino acids of which one, cysteine, is produced from homocysteine. The other two are glycine and glutamic acid. Peptides are abundant in your cells. Many message-carrying molecules such as ACTH and endorphins are peptides. RG is the most abundant and widely distributed peptide of them all and it has many jobs, most of them having to do with protecting you from oxidative damage and detoxification. It also works on several construction crews, synthesizing or forming larger molecules out of smaller ones. The most important thing to remember about RG's activities is that when RG detoxifies substances that are produced by your own metabolism (domestic waste, so to speak), it is able to transport the unwanted molecules to the outside and then return for another load. If, however, the toxic load is from the external environment (lead, cadmium, or mercury, for example), then RG has to take the load to the dump and stay there, never to return. RG is expensive; its presence depends on a metabolically costly and potentially dangerous means of production. The result is that for every atom of toxic substances that you consume and later need to get rid of, you are asking reduced glutathione to take a one-way trip to the dump.

5. Finally, RG has another job: tending a fire that is needed to create important messenger molecules called leukotrienes. Its job at the dump and protecting molecules from free radicals gives it an insider's understanding of the dangers of oxidation. RG directs one of the few operations in which oxidative forces are needed to create a new molecule.

Meanwhile, back at the Royal Court, we were in the process of seeing how Queen Methionine could regain her sovereignty by getting the methyl she gave up through her activities in the guise of SAM. Remember that SAM is busy distributing methyls around the body and, in particular, with the help of folic acid, to DNA where the methyls are needed for synthesis and repair. The restoration of methionine from homocysteine now depends on folic acid, working in conjunction with vitamin B_{12} and vitamin B_6. A lack of sufficient amounts of folic acid to accomplish this task implies a dual threat to your organism. The first is the potential for the buildup of homocysteine and the second is the potential for insufficient folic acid to repair DNA with the consequence of chromosome damage. Cancer arises in tissues that are busy being constantly renewed, such as the mucous membrane of the lungs and the digestive, urinary, and reproductive tracts when the supply of reparative methyls fails for lack of folic acid.[5]

It is probably not helpful, however, to keep focusing on cancer as the risk to be avoided. There are plenty of other things that can go wrong long before something turns into cancer. The implications for functional impairment in cognition, reproduction, and vitality in general are likely to be more widespread than the risk of cancer per se. Current medical technology does not have very good ways of measuring the impairment. The reason for covering this fairly complex branch of the chemistry of detoxification and repair is that it will become the hot new issue over the next few years. It has a bearing on the two major chronic illnesses of our culture: cardiovascular disease and malignancies. It is more important than cholesterol; however, detoxification is at the same stage as was cholesterol research twenty years ago. Eventually, the cholesterol research led to the development of drugs to lower cholesterol, and the medical profession was educated by the pharmaceutical industry to take a sharper look at cholesterol as a risk factor for cardiovascular disease. Problems of homocysteine and related chemistry will turn out to be more important to illness prevention than cholesterol ever was, but at the moment and for the foreseeable future the main remedies for individuals with the problem are nutritional supplements. This bodes poorly for patients in a medical environment that still categorizes nutrients as wimpy compared to pharmaceuticals.

Suppose you have a positive Pap smear, or perhaps a persistently positive Pap smear with extra worries and biopsies. Or suppose you have been a cigarette smoker or have been exposed to secondhand tobacco smoke. Or suppose that you have a history of inflammatory bowel disease or have a family history of bowel cancer. Or suppose that you are just plain paranoid about getting cancer. What can you do to protect your DNA from the difficulties repairing oxidative damage that constitutes part of the setup for cancer? At the risk of over-focusing I would like to highlight one of the simplest and safest things you can do: take a supplement of folic acid. How much? At least 400 mcg per day, but the dose for many people may be higher. I take 5,000 mcg (5 mg) daily, and I have seen many patients with persistent abnormal Pap smears that became normal only with daily doses in the 10- to 20-mg* range.

If you go to the health food store, you cannot obtain folic acid in doses greater than 800 mcg per pill. You can order folic acid from www.emersonecologics.com in higher doses.

You should not take folic acid if any of these factors exists:

- It disagrees with you (in any way). This is rare, but I have seen everything from changes in hair texture to depression reactions in individuals in whom the reasons behind their intolerance remained obscure.
- You are receiving certain kinds of chemotherapy treatments, such as methotrexate, aimed at harming the folic acid chemistry of the cancer cells. (But you can take folic acid when taking methotrexate for arthritis and other conditions in which the combination may enhance the treatment. And you may take folic acid when it is given as part of cancer treatment and given at a certain time of night according to your doctor's instructions.)
- You are unaware that taking it could make a hidden vitamin B_{12} deficiency worse.

This last reason is the basis for medical worries about unsupervised large doses of folic acid. Mind you, I think that if a large population of people all took folic acid supplements, far greater gains would be made than the losses in health of a few people who did not cover their B_{12} base. You can cover your base in the following ways. First, if you take large doses of folic acid without knowing your B_{12} status, you should keep that factor in mind should any new symptom arise, and be sure to point it out to your doctor. Second, you could take gener-

---

*1 mg = 1,000 mcg.

ous doses of vitamin B_{12}—say 1,000 mcg per week—by mouth, so that if you have a mild B_{12} absorption problem, you could overcome it with the large oral doses. Third, you could take a test for B_{12} to make sure you are not taking folic acid while already suffering from a B_{12} deficiency.

None of these plans is perfect but the third is the best. The reason it isn't quite perfect is that the tests for B_{12} are not perfect. The ordinary blood test for B_{12} as done at nearly every lab does not distinguish between pseudo-B_{12} made in your gut by your intestinal germs—but not of any use to you—and real B_{12}, such as you obtain from eating animal products (meat, milk, eggs, fish). One lab, Vitamin Diagnostics, Inc. (Route 35 & Industrial Drive, Cliffwood Beach, NJ 07735; Phone: 732-583-7773), is able to measure true B_{12} levels by a method developed by Herman Baker, Ph.D., in the 1970s. Another way of assessing vitamin B_{12} status is by measuring blood or urine levels of a naturally occurring chemical in your body called methylmalonic acid. Levels of methylmalonic acid rise with unmet B_{12} needs, which makes it the most sensitive test of B_{12} function in your body. Could some part of your body, such as your precious brain, be B_{12} deficient even if your blood or urine show no problem? Apparently the answer is yes.

In 1971 I sneered (slightly), as only a recently trained doctor can sneer, at my mentor and senior partner Paul Lavities, M.D., at the Community Health Care Plan in New Haven when I saw him giving a shot of B_{12} to an elderly woman. Wasn't that naturally bright red stuff just a placebo, sneered I? "No," said Dr. Lavities, a model practitioner of medicine as both an art and a science, "it really works."

It works in two ways. One is as a diagnostic trial, to see if a convincing response to it adds information that is not gained by lab tests. The other is as a therapeutic tool in many people who feel its benefit despite contradictory laboratory documentation. Thirty years ago my sneers were based on the then-accepted notion that the tests were decisive. Nowadays it turns out that no lab test is entirely decisive and we cannot do better than to believe the patient who describes or shows a benefit from its use, which must, at first anyway, be given by injection because the whole point about B_{12} is that its path for getting from your food to your bloodstream is unlike that of any other nutrient and very susceptible to failure.

The bottom line is that a modicum of thought and care is needed before taking large amounts of folic acid, but sparing a modicum of thought and care over this issue could easily spare your life. You will not see prime-time advertisements for folic acid. When you see your doctor, he or she will not have just been gifted a ballpoint pen emblazoned with folic acid from a sales rep. When your doctor, who does not believe in vitamins, orders fairly routine tests for folic acid, it is to spot an outright deficiency, not to measure whether you have the full protection for optimum repair of your treasured DNA.

The fullest protection for optimum repair of your DNA by the lights of contemporary science can only be provided by winging it with a generous supplement of folic acid, preferably taken at bedtime, because night is the time your body does growth, regeneration, and repair.

9

Understanding, Testing, and Treating Detoxification Chemistry

RETURNING FROM LUNCH to my cottage I spotted a monarch butterfly boldly flitting and gliding on the July breeze across the meadow. I say boldly because the meadow is inhabited by birds who would gladly make a meal of any number of passing insects including most butterflies. Not, however, of a monarch, one of the most poisonous creatures to travel the meadows of North America where it migrates annually thousands of miles to and from its winter home in Mexico. Poisons in the monarch's milkweed meals during its caterpillar stages accumulate in its body, neither being detoxified nor cast off during the transformation from larval stages to the winged adult. The poisons are safely sequestered in the wings, the least metabolically active parts of the butterfly, so that they harm only whatever animal might attempt to eat it. Thus, the monarch carries poisons as its license to parade its beauty in public with little danger of being eaten. A bird who takes only one less-than-deadly taste of a monarch will remember its mistake six months later and refuse any such meal again.[1] The monarch, like many insects, takes advantage of the poisonous nature of its host plant, the milkweed. Except for certain mechanisms for spreading their seeds, plants, in general, do not want to be eaten. Consider the millions of different kinds of plants on earth and the relatively small number that we humans are able to eat, and then remember that even those are not completely free of toxins. To be a plant is to be toxic in some way as part of a mechanism, however attenuated in some species, of self-protection. I have often watched my goats eat. They browse in the fields and woods with a careful preference for certain leaves that they can sniff out with a gourmet's discrimination. Their menu is much more varied than mine, in which very few leaves are represented. The goats have germs high up in their digestive processes, which not only digest cellulose but detoxify many of the substances in plants that could never be tolerated in animals that lack a rumen.

We humans have neither the front-end protection of a stomach full of cleaver germs or the downstream capability of sequestering toxins in our body, although we do have a minor talent for putting some toxic metals into our hair bound to the same sticky sulfur atoms that fasten the stranded molecules in position in each hair shaft. How then, do we deal with unwanted substances that get into us via our food, water, and air? How can we measure how many toxins we have accumulated and, more important, how can we test the efficiency of our detoxification machinery, the biggest part of our biochemistry?

Detoxification—a Costly Process

Let me elaborate on the last point before returning to follow some sample toxins through the system. One of the main points of this book is that some of the most troublesome toxins are ones that look so much like friendly molecules that they escape detection until they have already done mischief by masquerading as invited participants in a key biochemical step. You might expect that there is a major distinction between the way the body handles these substances and the friendly ones they mimic and the way it handles recognizably unwanted molecules, such as lead or various plant toxins. I have already said in Chapter 8 that reduced glutathione, one of the princely members of our family of detoxification chemicals, is *lost* from the body when a foreign chemical is detoxified while it is *recovered* from detoxification operations when the toxic substances are generated from our own chemistry. Otherwise everything in the body—all the molecules left over from the daily operations of the brain, bowels, blood, bones, muscles, skin, and all the internal organs—requires the use of the same chemistry that is used for dealing with naturally occurring toxins as well as with the environmental pollutants that enter with our food, water, and air. That is why cleansing the body of unwanted substances is the most costly metabolic activity in which our chemistry engages.

For a child, the cost of growth is also very high, but in adults, detoxification is the major molecule-making activity. That's right, *molecule-making*. Detoxification in human beings mostly involves synthesis as opposed to degradation. Even detoxification jobs that look as if they are mostly breaking things down turn out, in the end, to involve costly steps in which new molecules are made just for the sake of safe disposal. Take, for example, the detoxification of amino acids from the recycling of your tissue protein. Amino groups, removed from their amino acid or protein origins, turn into ammonia—the same strong poison that you recognize by its noxious odor. Ammonia cannot simply be allowed to go free inside your cells or in your blood. It is captured by alpha ketoglutarate (AKG), which becomes glutamate. Glutamate can take on another ammonia to become glutamine, which, in turn, delivers the unwanted ammonia to the single most expensive chemical department in the body, the urea cycle, where an elaborate process of handing off the ammonia is carried out with the final formation of urea, which can safely pass through the kidneys and out of the body. The breaking down of each amino acid molecule eventually requires making a molecule. The making of molecules for detoxification requires the lion's share of all the energy we expend on making any kind of molecule every day.

We go about our daily chores without conscious attention to the molecular details of our body's management of toxins, allergens, and other waste, but if our sanitation department did make itself known to us—say, by making a noise—it would drown out all the comparable noises of walking, thinking, and talking. Imagine the machinery of detoxification, mostly in the liver, emitting an enormous grinding, groaning, gurgling sound that would dwarf our loudest intestinal rumblings and belches. Considering that most detoxification goes on at night, the noise of our sanitation department would surely keep us up if it were able to give forth sounds comparable to the work it does. As it is, a faulty detoxification system is a common reason for poor sleep. We sometimes reach too quickly for a sedative for our nerves when it is our liver that needs help.

To understand the substantial portion of our daily expenditure of energy on all the chores of living that require making new molecules, consider how it would go if the body were a municipality. The budget would look like this:

Sanitation, 80 percent (the various detoxification activities)
Police, 5 percent (the immune system)
School system, 10 percent (the central nervous system)
Public works, 6 percent (maintenance of organs)

Do not hold me to the exact figures except that the sanitation figure is, if anything, a conservative estimate. With a child who is devoting energy to making new molecules every day to grow, the budget would allocate relatively more for public works. No matter how you slice it, however, it is sobering to realize that most of the molecules we synthesize every day are made for the sake of getting rid of waste molecules.

A Two-Step Operation

Before leaving the municipal analogy, let me make another general point about detoxification chemistry in preparation for a closer look at the details. It is a two-step operation. In my town the trash collection is done privately. For about a dollar a day, Harry Brasslett comes twice a week and takes away the trash, and on the second Wednesday of each month he comes for the recycling of bottles, cans, newspaper, and cardboard. Like detoxification chemistry, the semiweekly trash and the monthly recycling are each two-phase operations. Phase 1 consists of making the trash easy to pick up. I place it in barrels or in plastic sacks and put it in a convenient location, protecting it from the raccoons until a few hours before Harry makes his rounds. In phase 2 Harry comes in his big white truck and takes it away. The success of the operation depends not only on the timely preparation of the trash but on a certain balance between the capacities of each phase. When we need to get rid of unwanted molecules from our bodies the first phase renders the molecules easy to pick up. "Sticky" is a better image. A system of enzymes called cytochrome P450 prepares leftover or toxic molecules and affects the molecules in a way that is very roughly like rubbing a balloon on a sweater. At this moment the molecules that have been made more sticky, or "activated," are more dangerous than they were to begin with. A sticky toxin is not something you want banging around in your chemistry. It is like flypaper in the barn. It is good to have the flies stick to the paper, but if the paper gets stuck in your hair, it is worse than the flies were to begin with. The next step, then, is the timely appearance of the "Harry" molecules that carry the toxins away after safely containing them in a big white truck. Actually the process is called conjugation, and the more accurate image is sticking the sticky trash to individually tiny, somewhat sticky trucks. When each activated toxic or leftover molecule is stuck to a carrier molecule, it becomes deactivated and more soluble in the water of your blood or bile so that it can leave your body via your kidneys or intestine.

The carrier molecules (the tiny trucks) owe their stickiness to properties familiar to anyone who has experience with sugar or garlic. In fact, two of the main carrier molecules are sticky because they are like sugar: one comes directly from sugar (glucuronide), and the other is an amino acid (glycine) that is sweet and sticky like sugar. Two other carrier molecules owe their stickiness to the same feature that makes garlic peels adhere to your fingers: sulfur. Sulfur is stinky and sticky. Sulfur atoms appear wherever stickiness is needed in chemistry, so they have an adhesive function in building strong tissues and sticking to waste molecules in your body's sanitation department.

The brimstone appearing in bright yellow deposits around the fumaroles of volcanoes is sulfur. It has unique properties. It is the only naturally occurring substance found lying about on the planet that can burn, but was not once alive. Other elements oxidize; that is, they combine with the oxygen in the air as in the tarnishing of silver or the rusting of iron. Still other elements, such as sodium and potassium, burn explosively so that if they are removed from the liquid in which they are stored in a chemistry lab and plunged directly into a flushing toilet, the ensuing blast will cause serious damage to the plumbing. But sodium and potassium are not just lying around on the planet. In nature they are tightly combined with other elements to form compounds (such as table salt: sodium and chlorine), which are quite harmless because of a mutual neutralization of the chemical ferocity of the two components.

The chemical ferocity of sulfur, however, is special. It has an avidity for other elements that is more in keeping with the kinds of avidity that hold together living flesh. It is a nonliving substance that has the character of living or once-living material: it burns. As such it has "the imponderable qualities of life, light, warmth"[2] and, indeed, it is indispensable to life and a critical component of the diet. If the body does not get enough of it, or if it misuses it, the detoxification systems and the synthesis and repair of tissue are impaired. Remember Queen Methionine. Her treasure consists of methyl groups as well as sulfur. Methionine is one of the principal ways that sulfur enters the body to become the most important adhesive that holds it together and helps it safely get rid of your toxins and leftovers.

Testing Your Detoxification Chemistry

Remember my municipal analogy for detoxification in which the sanitation department used 80 percent of the town's budget to get rid of the garbage, trash, sewage, commercial and industrial waste, and stuff left behind by visitors from outside? In terms of energy spent on making new molecules, your body's budget devotes similar percentages to making detoxification molecules. By detoxification molecule, I mean one that combines a molecule of something your body is trying to get rid of with a carrier molecule, such as reduced glutathione, which helps usher it from the body. I am repeating this point because it is central to understanding how evaluation of detoxification chemistry fits in when assessing your health. Sick people have poor detoxification chemistry and people with poor detoxification chemistry tend to become sick. Moreover, detoxification chemistry is quite easy to repair.

If you, the reader, are a health practitioner, you know the pleasure that comes from seeing lab results get better as a result of your treatment. If you have not tested and treated abnormalities of detoxification chemistry, you can expect to be pleased when you do. It is really quite simple because the chemistry itself is straightforward and the treatment is rational, safe, and quickly effective.

On my way to describing the main test for detoxification chemistry, let me mention tests that may or may not provide clues to problems in detoxification. Analysis of your blood or urine for solvents or pesticides, or provocative tests for lead or mercury that show an excess body burden of toxins imply that your detoxification chemistry has not kept up with demand. Such tests do not, however, assess the capacity of your liver and other organs to do the job, and therefore do not distinguish between excess exposure and decreased detoxification capacity.

Because your liver is your main detoxification organ, you might expect a liver function profile to give you a good picture of your detoxification capabilities. However, a so-called liver function or liver profile test is *not* a sensitive indicator of the liver's capacity to rid itself of toxins. It can be a good early indicator of mischief caused by taking a medication or damage from alcohol or other toxins, but this profile is more of a liver damage test than a liver function test if the function in question is detoxification.

Testing of the two phases of detoxification is done with probes. In this sense, a probe is a chemical that is sent into the body by being swallowed or injected and then retrieved in a blood or urine specimen. Changes or lack thereof in the probe molecule can tell us about the way our body handles the probe or a whole class of substances of which the probe is a representative. Relatively innocent toxins can be used as probes to show how your body handles other toxins that are too dangerous to be administered as part of a test. The detoxification probes are caffeine, acetaminophen (Tylenol), and aspirin. Here is how it works. Each one of these substances acts like a sample of different classes of toxins that are disposed of by different processes by your body. By knowing how much you have taken and then measuring in your saliva (caffeine) or urine (aspirin and acetaminophen) the detoxified form of each, a good estimate can be made of the efficiency of the chemistry for handling these, and most other toxins and by-products of your metabolism. The test involves taking the three probes and then collecting saliva, urine, and sometimes blood for measurement. Great Smokies Diagnostic Laboratory provides all the materials necessary for the test as well as a clearly illustrated report of the results. This test is a real bargain: the basic version does not require you to have blood drawn, and it assesses the efficiency of major parts of your body's most metabolically costly biochemical department. Its results are logical and lead to specific, harmless treatment. And, in an otherwise well-nourished, infection-free person the treatment usually works quickly to restore the chemistry to normal.

The test measures the success of four phase 2 "ushers" in their task of linking up with toxins to carry them out of the body. Different people have different styles in the way they use these carrier molecules, so your test may show you to be below par in one of them but above par in another. If that is the case, you need not worry so long as the numbers for hooking up toxins with reduced glutathione sulfate, glucuronide, and glycine are robust.

Specific parts of the following protocol of supplements are aimed at abnormalities of various parts of the detoxification test. When one or more detoxification steps are weak and not balanced by strength in others, I tend to prescribe the whole protocol, which rarely fails to bring the test results to normal when remeasured after a month or so.

Supplement name	Approximate adult dose	Supplier	Comment	Possible side effects
Magnesium aspartate	3	Thorne	Each pill has 90 mg of magnesium as its aspartate salt. The reason for the supplement in this use is to deliver the aspartate, not the magnesium.	Loose stools—related to the magnesium
UltraClear	1 scoop	Metagenics		
Magnesium glycinate	3	Metagenics 900 mg glycine plus 100 mg of magnesium		Loose stools—related to the magnesium
Niacin time release	1	Thorne Niasafe—inositol hexaniacinate 600 mg or Twin Lab 800 mg hexanicotinate		
Pyridoxal 5 phosphate 50 mg	2	This is a form of vitamin B_6		

Do not just take these supplements and conclude that if they make you feel better you must have had poor detoxification. The detoxification profile is a prime exception to the rule that your body is the best laboratory. I know of few tests showing problems that are more important and easy to fix, yet tend to yield less in terms of immediate relief of specific symptoms. The failure of repair of detoxification chemistry to give quick results the way, say, treatment of iron deficiency does is puzzling to me. I'm also puzzled when people ask, "If my detoxification chemistry is broken, how should I feel?" These would be tougher questions to answer if most people were not already aware of preventive health measures. Lowering your intake of refined sugars and saturated fat, raising your intake of omega-3 oils, reducing caffeine intake, and taking supplements of folic acid and other nutrients bring more long-term than short-term benefits for most people. So it is with repair of detoxification chemistry. This means that there is even more reason to understand the detoxification deal. I believe that as this deal is more widely understood among professionals and laypeople, detoxification testing will become a routine part of screening apparently healthy people, as it should now be a part of assessing people with symptoms. To summarize, detoxification is one of your body's biggest jobs. Failure to do it well can get you into trouble, testing it is simple, and fixing it is easy. Seems like a pretty good deal to me.

I hope you have noticed that I have skipped saying much about assessing and correcting problems in phase 1 of detoxification. Recall that phase 1 is where toxins as well as the leftovers from your own metabolism are rendered sticky so that the usher molecules, also sticky, can grab them with final efficiency and take them away. Phase 1 is carried out by a family of enzymes known as the cytochrome P450 system, which includes various specialists for giving stickiness to different kinds of molecules. No single probe would test for all the possibilities. Most candidate molecules are simply too toxic to consider taking for the sake of evaluating your phase 1. So we are stuck with caffeine, the fate of which in your detoxification system gives a good, but imperfect idea of how phase 1 is doing. I'll finish this chapter with a story that focuses on this point and elaborates on the risks of ignoring detoxification chemistry.

Terry Handler is a talented, loveable, overweight, divorced forty-four-year-old man who works part-time in a health food store. He has never loved himself and has not lived up to his talents. Since childhood, most of his efforts have been devoted to coping with a confusing mix of problems:

- Muscle spasms that awaken him at night
- Difficulty concentrating, which caused school failure in the past
- Abdominal bloating, gas, and diarrhea
- Obsessive-compulsive habits, such as having to repeatedly check the garbage to be sure he didn't discard something by mistake
- Excessive sweating
- Depression
- Burning sensation on the soles of his feet
- Fatigue

His symptoms improved over the first few years of treatments that included balancing his bowel flora, correcting a magnesium deficiency, and supplements of essential fatty acids. Then things stalled. He had numerous silver-mercury amalgam fillings and ate tuna four times weekly. I suggested that he get his amalgam fillings removed. Over a five-day period of DMSA loading (see Chapter 6) his urine mercury level rose from a high baseline of 9.1 to 26 mcg per twenty-four hours and his lead from a normal baseline of 1.6 to 19.1. Although he initially felt worse while taking DMSA, he continued taking repeated courses of it. He experienced a dramatic change in his health, with major improvements in all of his symptoms. He also returned to school, where he got A's in all his courses.

During this initial treatment he continued to turn out such a remarkable amount of lead and mercury that we reviewed his history in detail to see if we could spot a past exposure. Failing that, I looked at his detoxification profile, which yielded a result of zero for phase 1. I had not previously seen a result of zero in a test that usually shows numbers from 0.5 to 1.6 and, in people who have a heavy exposure to toxins, may be quite elevated in response to that exposure. Figuring that the lab had made an error, I asked Terry to repeat the test and got the same result.

I suggested that Terry take a supplement (Indolplex, six daily) of DIM (substances extracted from cruciferous plants such as cabbage, broccoli, brussels sprouts, and cauliflower), which works to improve phase 1. The combination of DIM supplementation and periodic three-day courses of DMSA have made a big difference in Terry's symptoms.

The lessons I learned from Terry's experience are:

1. In people with complex chronic illness, the role of mercury from diet (fish) and fillings (silver-mercury amalgam) should be considered high, not low, on the list of considerations.
2. When the history of exposure fails to reveal enough to account for lead or mercury recovered during treatment, be especially aware of the possibility of a defect in detoxification.
3. Some individuals feel so much better during and immediately after DMSA treatment that their response becomes a good indicator of further need for treatment. When that happens, one does not know for sure whether the response is entirely due to heavy metal removal or to other biochemical benefits of DMSA.

Here is another story from a patient whose detoxification issues taught me a lesson worth passing on.

When I first met Ann Wheeler twenty years ago, she was the forty-eight-year-old mother of one of my patients and grandmother-to-be of two more. She was young looking, fit, and healthy, except for multiple food and chemical sensitivities. Addressing her yeast problem brought these under control, and she remained free of symptoms so long as she was careful about environmental exposures. She moved to a pollution-free part of the country and built a house that minimized her exposure to chemicals.

In 1998, Ann developed breast cancer. We reviewed her risk factors, which included the kinds of emotional traumas (loss) that are sometimes associated with cancer risk. Toxic exposures seemed unlikely. We were both surprised when blood tests showed very high levels of *n*-hexane and 3-methylpentane, petrochemicals that appeared to come from exposure to gasoline (not exhaust from its combustion). She subjected her car, her home, her well, and every possible other source of exposure to exacting scrutiny and she and I both sought the advice of environmental experts. After checking things out, she decided that the absence of any exposure was enough to reassure her that she was not in any jeopardy. It was harder for me to give up on the fact that unexplained lab test reports were sitting in her file. They had been repeated for confirmation, and I was left with a quandary.

After several months, it finally dawned on me that I had, in my friend Jon Pangborn, Ph.D., an expert resource I had failed to tap. Founder of Bionostics, a biochemical consulting service, Jon had started his career as a petroleum chemist—the kind who can tell from a whiff of your exhaust whether your car is burning fuel that originated beneath Texas or Kuwait. Jon pointed out that intestinal germs produce various inflammable hydrocarbons, starting with methane, and also including pentane and hexane. These vapors emerge in stools and flatus as well as being susceptible to absorption into the bloodstream. Eureka! A short course of bovine colostrum-derived transfer factor brought Ann's blood hydrocarbon levels to normal. Colostrum is the substance mammals produce for the education of their offspring's immune systems with molecules that are too big to pass across the placenta that serves as the interconnection between mother and baby before birth. The breast from the time of birth for a few days before milk starts being produced secretes colostrum. Colostrum contains, among other substances, molecules that help the baby sort out the germs that will inhabit its digestive tract beginning within hours of birth and accumulating, in the case of human babies, with exposure to the germ population of those handling the baby in the first weeks of life, mainly the mother. The germs of most mammals' digestive tracts are similar, so the colostrum harvested from cows can be used to help the human intestinal tract accept good germs and reject bad ones. This function is of value not only to babies who may have been deprived of breast-feeding but also to infants and adults whose intestinal germ population has gotten out of balance after antibiotic treatment.

We still don't know whether these findings had anything to do with her breast cancer risk factors. The question involves more than just knowing whether exposure to such hydrocarbons is a factor in cancer risk. The answer is both simple and complex. The simple part is that abnormalities in bowel flora are linked to breast cancer. The complicated part is knowing whether bowel flora changes that are known to affect estrogen metabolism may have been, in Ann, associated with the findings of hexane and pentane in her blood. The bowel flora–estrogen question is reviewed in my book *The Circadian Prescription* (Putnam Perigee, 2000).

The Role of Oxidative Stress

Most of the tests I have referred to so far measure a kind of problem that can be localized to a particular place in the body or its digestive, immune, and biochemical processes. What about testing for damage by oxidative stress, which could show up anywhere from the fatty acids in sunburned skin on the tip of the nose to the nucleic acids in the DNA of cells that are destined for conceiving a child? Oxidative damage, the loss of electrons from molecules that lose a tug-of-war with oxygen or other electron-hungry thieves, takes place everywhere, but its effects might be felt in different ways depending on the life span and location of, say, the skin cells or the reproductive system. As I described previously, the fatty acids of the cell membranes are some of the most susceptible to the theft of their electrons. Packed together like millions of caterpillars standing on their tails, the oxidation of one of them yields a domino effect among its neighbors. The magnification of damage caused by the domino effect makes fatty acids (also known under the collective term *lipids*) good objects of analysis to see how much oxidative stress the body has endured without being able to defend itself with the team of antioxidants, including vitamin C, the flavonoids, beta-carotene, vitamin E, and reduced glutathione. Just as I pointed out that this partnership of chemicals works as a team, it is appropriate to neither give one team member alone as a treatment nor to measure one member as a way of assessing the efficiency of the whole team. Consequently we either need to measure all of these substances, which can be done in a blood specimen, or we can measure the effect of the team's failure. Blood tests for rancid fatty acids (or lipid peroxides) are the best direct measure of oxidative damage. Another good test involves adding a step to the detoxification test I described earlier in which caffeine, acetaminophen, and aspirin are run through the system to see how well they are detoxified. If blood as well as urine is used for analysis, the by-products of the body's handling of aspirin can be used to assess the degree of oxidative stress inside cells.

The development of the aspirin test for oxidative stress as well as future tests[3] to evaluate other key indicators of cellular health and oxidative stress (e.g., nitric oxide) is largely the work of Jeffrey Bland, Ph.D. Between the lines of this book you can find the birth record of a new paradigm of medicine that is coming into being. Dr. Bland has been the principal midwife of this delivery. He has been and continues to be the preeminent educator of physicians whose appetite for biochemistry and immunology has been whetted by their need to study their patients as individuals. Thousands of patients have benefited directly from the knowledge that Dr. Bland has brought to their physicians with a flawless sense for applying a rigorous, detailed understanding of biochemistry to a systems approach to medicine and a superlative knack for explaining things.

10

Fat Is Not Just to Hold Up Your Pants

When Zack was eighteen years old he took a trip with his dad to Central America. It was, in part, a continuation of a connection that had taken them on many adventures. It was also a celebration of Zack's growing independence. The price of freedom is higher for children growing up with illness. No other illness exacts its price with such intensity as autism. Zack has autism. Autism ties him up, restricts the movements of his thought to repetitious efforts, and distorts his attention so that he finds fascination in a word or image that seems to come out of left field. He had done pretty well in college considering that getting to know a lot of new people is not easy for anyone who is unable to read faces (or the feelings at work behind the faces). Zack took a semester off from college. The trip was a break from all of that and a reward for having given it a really good try and wanting to try again.

Zack and his dad saw the sights, swam, fished, went out to dinner, and had a great time until Zack had a meltdown on the day they left. They were at a small airport, with a big plane waiting. Soldiers, police, immigration, and security men displayed force not familiar to North Americans at that time. There was no line, just 300 people waiting like candy in a gumball machine. Zack started screaming, yelling, and hitting himself on the head. "I want my freedom," he yelled as the crowd jumped back and the law moved in. The handcuffs came off more than an hour later after Zack's father's apologies and explanations hit home with the officer who had been called to sort things out. Zack had been immediately remorseful, saying, "I have never been this autistic before." He had another episode on the plane. Once home he began having such outbursts with increasing frequency. The circumstances were varied and did not seem to be linked by connecting threads. He even attacked his dear housekeeper. I had been getting to know Zack, his biochemistry, immunology, and his dad for nine years. It took quite a lot of effort for me to refocus on someone I knew so well and take a fresh history. A detail gave me a clue. The skin on the backs of Zack's hands had become dry and cracking to the point of bleeding, and his dandruff had gotten worse coincident with the appearance of his tantrums. Tantrums can come from many causes, but tantrums and dry skin usually come from a deficiency of omega-3 fatty acids. Dry skin without tantrums usually comes from such a deficiency and tantrums without dry skin can too. The combination is a giveaway. I prescribed a very generous supplement of omega-3 oils in the form of one tablespoon of cod liver oil and two tablespoons of flax oil in addition to the supplement of two capsules of Udo's oil, a proprietary supplement of omega-3 oils that Zack had been taking for a few years. His tantrums stopped over the next few weeks and have not returned. When I learned about OmegaBrite (see page 181), I added six capsules a day to Zack's regimen. I had not been sure that the oils' intervention would work, but my experience with tantrums over the past twenty years keeps omega-3 oils near the top of my list. My only surprise was that Zack's needs exceeded the maintenance supplement that he had been taking right along.

Sandra Tiepolo was the sister of a long-standing patient who called me in distress to report that Sandra had a cancerous lesion discovered at the opening of her vagina. Her doctor was considering very extensive surgery that would have left Sandra crippled as far as sex and reproduction were concerned. The lesion was indeed a very scary-looking, cancerous one. In addition, Sandra had severe dandruff, dry skin, brittle fingernails, chicken skin on the backs of her arms, and alligator skin on her legs. She was a catalog of the physical signs of omega-3 fatty acid deficiency. I suggested that Sandra begin to replenish her oils while watching her lesion very closely and deferring surgery as long as some immediate improvement was noted. She took a tablespoon or two of flaxseed oil daily. Within days her dandruff began to clear, as did the other signs of fatty acid deficiency. Within a couple of weeks her cancerous lesion began to regress, and it disappeared over the ensuing thirteen months. The happy ending is that Sandra subsequently married and had a daughter who is a teenager now.

Could you get any further apart than a story about meltdowns in an autistic young man and a cancer scare in a young woman? These two conditions are so different that medical scientists and ordinary people might be downright offended by the idea that some panacea would treat both. A panacea is a universal remedy, something that is good for everything. The medical profession is skeptical about panaceas. Modern medicine practice has advanced on particularizing illnesses, each of which has its own remedy. It would be silly to suggest that the same remedy would work for very different acute problems, such as a broken arm, a case of strep throat, and a facial pimple on the day of the prom. Would it be so silly to suggest that the same remedy would work for different chronic illnesses such as depression, colitis, asthma, and eczema? It may help to consider this question by thinking of the remedy as something that is good not for every*thing* but for every*body*. It goes along with the idea that the person, not the disease, is the target of treatment.

The next phase of advancement in medical practice will come from particularizing not illness, but people. That is, delving into individuality in ways that permit directing treatment at individual imbalances as opposed to group conditions.

So how does it figure that those omega-3 fatty acid supplements are good for everybody if each of us is different? How does it figure that detailed tests for fatty acid imbalances are generally not necessary prior to prescribing fatty acids? Suppose you take a group of 100,000 people of all ages and submit them to an experiment in which you deprive them of omega-3 fatty acids over a period of fifty years. Among those 100,000 people would be groups with various tendencies toward developing depression, colitis, arthritis, asthma, eczema, cardiovascular disease, cancer, and the whole array of problems of which we are aware. The lowering of fatty acids in the whole population would be like the lowering of the tide in the harbor, exposing hidden rocks. Decreasing omega-3 fatty acid intakes in 100,000 people would expose some rocks in the form of dandruff and split ends and others in the form of manic-depressive illness or cancers depending on the genetic tendency and other environmental risk factors that our population endured. The fatty acid deficit would not be the *cause* of the skin, mood, and cancer problems—any more than the lowering tide caused the rocks. The deficit exposed problems that would never have happened to many in the population. Here is how it works.

Dr. Andrew Stoll, research director of Harvard University's McLean Hospital has proven that supplements of omega-3 fatty acids work better than drugs in helping people with bipolar disorder. One good scientific study can rescue the truth of many anecdotes. The value of omega-3 fatty acids has been proven with respect to problems in the bowel, joints, skin, and heart and now we have Dr. Stoll's studies to validate the anecdotal evidence for the oil-brain connection. Do Dr. Stoll's studies mean that Zack has bipolar disorder? No. Dr. Stoll's studies focus on a particular group of people who can be classified together for research purposes. The bipolar research showing the effectiveness of omega-3 oils to be greater than the drug lithium did not pay much attention to the skin or bowel problems of the patients participating in the studies. The focus was on the symptoms needed to qualify for the diagnosis under study. When Donald Rudin, M.D., first told me about his studies in the 1970s of oils in the treatment of people with serious mental problems, he did emphasize that skin problems provide a good handle on spotting people who may benefit from fatty acid supplementation. Dr. Stoll's studies serve as a reminder that people can have dramatic benefit from omega-3 oils whether or not they have skin signs, but let's start with the skin, which often provides the kind of clue that helped us sort out Zack's difficulties.

Signs of fatty acid problems—basically omega-3 oil deficiency—are among the most reliable among the subtle findings in the nutritional assessment of patients. For reasons I will explain in a moment these signs can be found in a large proportion of "normal" people as well as in those with a wide variety of health problems. Fatty acid chemistry is deep, and the way its abnormalities are reflected on the surface and in the symptoms of individuals can be quite varied. The clues that can be observed on the skin, however, fall into a spectrum in which a theme of dryness is manifested in different ways. They are:

1. Cracking fingertips—worse in winter
2. Patchy dullness of the skin, especially on the face, with a subtle patchy variation in the color of the skin
3. Mixed oily and dry skin, which, in cosmetic advertisements, is sometimes called combination skin
4. Chicken skin (*phrynoderma, hyperkeratosis follicularis*), which comprises small, rough bumps on the back of the arms
5. Alligator skin, usually on the lower legs, which develop an irregular quilted appearance with dry patches
6. Stiff, dry, unmanageable, brittle hair
7. Seborrhea, cradle cap, dandruff, hair loss
8. Soft fingernails or brittle fingernails that fray with horizontal splitting

These findings usually respond dramatically when a person takes a supplement of omega-3 oils. Associated symptoms, sometimes including severe problems, often melt away as the skin signs do. The variety of problems that respond to omega-3 fatty acid supplementation crosses all the boundaries between systems, specialties, and diseases. Most people who have skin signs of fatty acid problems use various kinds of lotions, oils, shampoos, conditioners, and cosmetics to cover their problems, often to no avail.

Why Oils Can Heal or Harm

How can it be that not eating, or eating, certain oils could make such a difference in people's health? The subject is very thoroughly covered in several good books, so I will only give you a summary and my particular viewpoint here. The toxicity of bad oils and the benefits of good oils represent a very different kind of problem in detoxification from all the others I describe in this book. The toxicity is far from poisoning in the sense of what happened to the ambassador's daughter, and yet I believe it is the most common kind of poisoning that a practicing physician can find in his or her patients today.

Most of us have been taught to think of fat as basically dangerous, something to be avoided for the sake of one's health. In my medical training, the chemistry of lipids, a more technical term for fats, received little attention. No other factor in nutrition has gone from such a lowly to such an exalted position as my understanding of the importance of oils to health. Fats and oils have three quite different roles in the body, two of which account for the major shift in my appreciation of the subject. The same two roles of fatty acids, as certain lipids are known, explain their enormous significance to health as exemplified in the cases I just described. After a brief description of each role of fatty acids, I will highlight a few key details.

1. The first role of fat is to hold up your pants, or otherwise provide the bulges and curves that belong to a well-rounded person. The fats and oils in your diet that become your body fat are an efficient form of stored energy. It is basically the only way the body has to store fuel that can carry you more than several hours beyond your last meal. Unlike plants, human beings do not have any way to store large amounts of carbohydrates to serve as stable reservoirs of energy. However, the liver does store some carbohydrate as glycogen that provides some energy during the initial day of a fast or during prolonged exercise. We can store fats, which some plants do as well. Nuts and seeds are the best example of plant stores of fat.
2. The second role of fat in your body is to make waterproof membranes. In this case I am not referring to membranes such as the surface of an organ or the mucous membranes lining the inner passageways of your body. I am referring to cell membranes. Your body is made of cells, which are units of life. Life goes on only in the watery environment inside cells, whose water has a special composition quite different from the water outside of cells, whether that be seawater in

the case of single-cell organisms, fresh water, or the water of your blood or in the spaces between the cells of complex organisms. Every cell is enclosed in a membrane that provides the waterproofing that enables it to separate its inside water from the water of its surroundings. The cell membrane is made of an uninterrupted fabric made of oil molecules.

3. The third role of oil molecules in your body is to become hormones. Usually, when you hear the word *hormone*, you think of substances such as thyroid hormone or estrogen, testosterone, cortisol, and other steroid hormones. Another category of hormones is less familiar to most people, partly because these, the prostanoid hormones, were discovered more recently (in the 1960s) and because they do not have an affiliation with a particular organ. Moreover, shortages of these hormones produce symptoms that do not fit as neatly into the picture of a disease as do shortages of the other well-known hormones. Prostanoid hormones are made exclusively from fatty acids.

Keep these three roles of fatty acids—energy storage, water-proofing cell membranes, and hormone synthesis—in mind as we explore the ways fatty acids can be toxic or beneficial.

You *Are* What You Eat

Our palate for oils is blunt. I am sure that there are chefs and gourmets who can taste-test olive oil and determine its provenance as can an experienced oenologist tell the year and vineyard of a particular wine. When it comes to oils, however, most of us can barely distinguish between samples of mineral oil, olive oil, safflower oil, flaxseed oil, and motor oil when they are presented to be sniffed, touched, and (except for the motor oil) tasted. I have experimented with audiences to demonstrate that we tend toward taste blindness when attempting to distinguish among the various oils. This is the reason the concept of "vegetable oil" or "salad oil" was readily accepted among Americans in the 1950s when corn and other oils came onto a market that previously offered only olive oil, lard, butter, and margarine. Even families with a solid tradition of using culinary olive oil could be persuaded to switch to various mongrel oils sold in the supermarket. Such oils, extracted from various plant seeds by means of hot steel rollers and a process that involves dissolving and recovering the oils from a solvent similar to dry-cleaning fluid, were sold with the assumption that this clear, pure-appearing stuff was what we consumers wished to (or could be made to wish to) eat. The oils were also marketed with an eye toward shelf life, so that a bottle of vegetable oil that languished on the shelf of the general store would not go bad over a period of months. Some of the oils that can be squeezed and dissolved out of, say, a corn kernel, are quite susceptible to spoilage while others are very stable. Removing the vulnerable fraction of the oil results in a product of remarkable stability. The problem is that the oils that are removed are nutritionally valuable, while the ones that remain are nutritionally undesirable or even toxic. Still, these altered oils may taste just fine. They are toxic not because they are rancid but because they have been altered to lengthen their shelf life. The result is a man-made oil that provides us with molecules we do not need and deprives us of those we do need. Our taste buds are hopeless at giving us the slightest clue that this has happened.

Toxic oils are probably the most important issue in human health in our time, but the effects of their toxicity are quite different from those presented by the other kinds of toxicity cited in this book. All you need to understand about oils and fats derives from three simple sets of facts.

1. **Whatever fats you eat become your fat.** I have just explained that our sense of taste can't discriminate between different kinds of oils and fats. They are so interchangeable as to be listed on labels of prepared foods as "one or the other of the following." The manufacturer is then free to use whatever source of shortening is currently most available or cheapest on the market. Whatever fats you eat become *your* fat. Contrary to the points I made in the previous chapter, dietary fats enter the fat stores and cell membranes without being

altered. If you eat chicken fat, your fat reflects the fatty acid composition of the chicken. If you were to eat only fat from olive oil, then your body's fat composition would reveal the distinctive proportions of the main fatty acids in olives. Unlike proteins and carbohydrates, dietary fatty acids come into the body by a very direct path and are neither identified nor, for the most part, disassembled and reassembled. On the other hand, the protein of your body is distinctively yours: if you eat cow's muscle or drink cow's milk, your muscle and your secretions still retain your own distinctive human composition. The same is true for carbohydrates.

The body is capable of making all kinds of fatty molecules that are similar to the ones in your diet (except for two), but usually it does not bother to do so; it uses the fat molecules (fatty acids) that you have eaten. After you swallow your food, the fats and oils are separated from the carbohydrate and protein as they pass through the upper part of the intestine. The carbohydrate, which is broken down into sugars, and the protein, which is broken down into amino acids, pass into the liver where they can be monitored for any properties that are foreign to your nature and altered accordingly. The fatty acids in the fat you eat go by an entirely different route directly from the digestive tract into the bloodstream. This path consists of a vessel that delivers all the fats and oils of your meal directly to a large blood vessel at the base of the neck just below the collarbone. The whole concept of digestion is therefore different as far as fats are concerned as compared with carbohydrate and protein. In the case of fats, their digestion is nondestructive and intended only to convert the fats and oils into tiny droplets that can float into the blood.

2. **The only two fats you cannot make, but have to get from food, are the raw materials for making a whole family of important hormones.** This is one of the most important scientific facts I have learned since before college when Mr. Mayo-Smith began to teach me biology beginning with the notion that there are a few pivotal facts that give

leverage to thinking. To recap: when it comes to fat, you are what you eat. Although the body has the capacity to make fat molecules on its own (for example, from sugar), it generally does not do so. However, there are two essential fatty acids that the body cannot make. The pivotal fact here is that these two fatty acid molecules are the exclusive raw materials for making *all* of the prostanoid hormones. Let me put it another way: the body has a constant need to synthesize and manufacture an assortment of substances called prostanoid hormones, the main vehicles for communication from cell to cell in the body. Unlike steroid hormones, which are synthesized in special glands (adrenals, ovaries, testicles), or thyroid hormones, which come exclusively from the thyroid gland, the prostanoid hormones are made by just about every cell in the body. Steroid and thyroid hormones are examples of long-distance message carriers originating in organs that are remote from the tissues throughout the body where their message is targeted. Prostanoid hormones are more involved with short-distance message carrying, and there is no special organ in the body that has the exclusive job of producing them.

A whole orchestra of prostanoid hormones is in constant production. Their combined effect is like music that cells play to their neighbors to keep their mutual efforts harmonized. All of the instruments of this music are made out of the two kinds of fat molecule that have to be eaten regularly to supply the necessary raw materials. It seems extraordinary to me that Mother Nature made us entirely dependent on our diet to supply these two molecules when we have a full capacity to produce at least a couple of dozen other molecules that differ from them in what appear to be only minor details.

The names of the two essential fatty acids are linoleic acid and alpha-linolenic acid. Omega-3 fatty acids are the family of fatty acids we make from alpha-linolenic acid. When the manufacturers of vegetable oil developed methods for squeezing various seeds to extract their oils, and various kinds of "salad" or "cooking" oils hit the market in the 1950s, the oils were able to survive on grocery shelves for months without becoming rancid because the manufacturers removed the alpha-linolenic acid, the oil that has the greatest tendency to rancidity. At the time, no one knew that linoleic acid and alpha-linolenic acid had crucial roles as the exclusive precursors of all of the prostanoid hormones. Prostanoid hormones would not be discovered, nor their chemistry unraveled, until more than a decade later.

3. **All of the cell membranes of the body are made of fatty acids. Cell membranes need to be flexible to function. The two fatty acids we cannot make are the flexible ones.** Their unique role in prostanoid hormone chemistry would be enough to place the role of fatty acids in hormone production among the top few items in my biochemical knowledge. However, the use of fatty acids for making cell membranes is a corollary fact that puts it at the very top. Life goes on in cells, not in the spaces in between. For all the cells (100,000,000,000,000 or 10^{13} of them) to function optimally, they must be able to communicate with each other. Prostanoid hormones are one of the most important means for such communication. Each individual cell must be open to such communication while at the same time it must be closed off from the water that surrounds it. The fabric of their waterproof membranes is a velvet made of fatty acids forming the nap. Each tiny strand that forms the surface of the velvet is a fatty acid, a long skinny molecule standing on its end amidst millions of others in all directions, each nested against the other like stacked spoons. One layer of fatty acid velvet faces inward to the inside of the cell and another faces outward, like two pieces of velvet with their naps facing. The whole arrangement owes its most important property (being waterproof) to the fact that oil and water do not mix. There is water inside the membrane

and water outside the membrane but the membrane itself does not get wet.

Unlike the cells of plants and fungi, the cell membrane is not a wall. It is a delicate diaphanous fabric with a flexibility more like silk than velvet. It must be so in order to accommodate one of the main functions of the membrane: communication. That is, it must be able to form various kinds of pockets in which protein and carbohydrate molecules float in the fat to be receptor sites for messenger molecules coming from other cells. For the cell membrane to be flexible it must be made of flexible oils. Which are the most flexible oils? You guessed it: linoleic acid and, especially, alpha-linolenic acid. Alpha-linolenic acid owes its flexibility to the same property that makes it vulnerable to giving up electrons and thus becoming oxidized or rancid; it is very unsaturated. Alpha-linolenic acid is the queen of the polyunsaturated fatty acids and the mother of the omega-3 family of fatty acids.

Essentially, all of the business of the body is conducted within membranes. Those that surround the cell, however important, are part of a much larger system of membranes inside each cell that support the activities of cellular life. If you were to take the measure of the surface membrane of each cell and multiply it by the number of cells in the body, the total surface area would be as large as a tennis court or two. As for the total surface area of all the membranes inside the cells, this would be about the size of ten football fields. It takes a lot of flexible fatty acids to keep these membranes flexible; this is crucial because the stiffer they are, the less well they work.

How does this flexibility—or lack thereof—manifest itself in your health? The stiff and weakening changes in hair, skin, and nails are easy to see in terms of the effects of a lack of fatty acids that have to do with flexibility. The changes that result in hormonal imbalances and cellular damage leading to cancer, heart disease, and other major problems are more difficult to visualize. Moreover, the chain of cause and effect is more complex than, say, the way a tick toxin or an egg allergy can cause illness. The complexity of understanding cause and effect increases as you are asked to make a distinction between bad fats and good fats. Simply put, the "good" fats are the thin ones that make flexible cell membranes and prostanoid hormones. The "bad" ones are the stiff ones, the altered oils from which the good fatty acids have been removed.

Fat can harm the body in three ways, two of which you cannot taste. The third, rancidity, tastes so unpleasant that your taste buds know how to protect you. Let's begin with the first two.

When vegetable oils are extracted and processed from seeds and nuts, two kinds of damage occur to their fatty acid molecules. The damage is related to two of the ways fat can go bad. In the first way, the pressure and heat of the extracting process causes some of the molecules to undergo rotation at one of their joints, where two carbon atoms have a double connection with each other. As a result, the molecules change shape. The curve that normally occurs at each double connection becomes reversed so that the molecule is straightened. Recall that in the cell membrane the molecules are nested together like stacked spoons. Straightened ones lose their capacity to fit together in the velvet of the cell membranes, just as a knife would not nest in a stack of spoons. The transformation into an unnatural, straightened fatty acid is one that technical terminology designates as a "trans" configuration. Except for those that are cold-pressed, processed oils tend to have more or less trans fatty acids, which stiffen the cell membranes. They are also unsuited for use as raw materials for making prostanoid hormones.

Margarine tends to have an especially high percentage of trans fatty acids. Margarine, however, is especially toxic for other reasons. Its oils have been intentionally altered and straightened by another process called hydrogenation. Hydrogenation consists of bubbling hydrogen through an oil under conditions in which hydrogen joins fatty acid molecules at the double connections between carbon atoms. The addition of the hydrogen atoms can occur only if half of the double connection is converted for hydrogen holding. Once the new hydrogen is added at these points, the double connections are lost as the fatty acid becomes more saturated with respect to hydrogen. The end result is an oil that has changed from thin and flexible to thick and stiff. The resulting thick and stiff oil resembles fats and oils that are naturally thick and stiff, such as one finds in fattened animals and in naturally saturated oils.

Thick and stiff oils are toxic in that they cause an unwelcome rigidity in cell membranes and do not provide suitable raw materials for making hormones. The symptoms, physical signs of dry skin or hair and the medical problems of the patients I described earlier can all be understood in terms of the effects of too many altered (trans or stiffened) fatty acids and an insufficiency of good, flexible oils.

The reason that flaxseed oil is especially medicinal for individuals who require an oil change is that it has an exceptional concentration (about 40 percent) of the thinnest, most flexible alpha-linolenic oil of all seeds and nuts. The next closest in concentration are walnuts and rapeseed, the source of canola oil. Each of these oils has about one-fourth the concentration of flaxseed oil. Flaxseed oil is a traditional food oil in parts of Eastern Europe such as the Ukraine. Its plant source is used for making linen cloth, and its small pointed brown seeds yield their oils when pressed by old-fashioned methods available before the modern hot steel rollers used today. Antioxidants are abundant in oils that are freshly pressed by old-fashioned methods that yield a turbid product that would seem dirty looking to the eye of consumers accustomed to transparent "pure" oils. The apparent "impurities" in these oils are actually parts of the crushed seed that contain the antioxidants that permit seeds to stay fresh during prolonged storage. Similarly, these antioxidants, such as vitamin E, protect the unrefined oil when stored or heated in ways that are not recommended for purified oils. Family members who grew up on old-fashioned flaxseed oil tell me that it would stay fresh all year without refrigeration and that its taste was much more agreeable than the flaxseed oils that are currently available in the United States. Flaxseed, or linseed, oil was used in Eastern European homes as the principal edible oil for cooking. It was also used medicinally for treating burns where its effectiveness may be due to its generous content of antioxidants. Its effectiveness in treating a wide variety of skin, hair, and nail problems and much deeper underlying medical disorders is owed to its capacity to restore flexibility to cell membranes and replenish the supply of the raw materials needed for prostaglandin hormone synthesis.

The most concise way of describing the superficial effects of restoring the body's supply of alpha-linolenic acid is to say that it gives luster. When we are in good health, we show a glow of health about us.

Such a glow is easily recognized but difficult to describe except that it has to do with the emission or reflection of light. It is no coincidence that flaxseed oil is the unique vehicle for oil paint pigments where it imparts a luster to paintings that cannot be duplicated by another oil. When a painter runs out of linseed oil, he or she does not accept substitution with olive, corn, or coconut oil. Neither should you. And, when your skin gets dull and dry, you should consider whether your oil needs changing before you reach for a cream, lotion, oil, or cosmetic to cover up the problem.

Are there tests to measure what you are missing? Serious alterations in the kinds of fatty acids in your blood and cell membranes can be detected by ordinary quantitative tests for fatty acids. Even so, such tests are available only at special laboratories.[1] Early stages of fatty acid deficiency are common in North Americans, who consume mostly altered or saturated fats. The analysis of blood to detect these abnormalities is the special interest of Dr. Eduardo Siguel, who has developed the technology to measure early changes in the proportions of good and bad fatty acids including Mead acid, which the body starts to make for use in cell membranes when it runs out of alpha-linolenic acid. Mead acid lacks the proper shape and flexibility of the real thing. However, it is all the body can do in a pinch and it is one of the keys to Dr. Siguel's method for fatty acid deficiency determination.[2] Dr. Siguel's book[3] provides a comprehensive review of the subject, and several of his recent papers describe essential fatty acid deficiency as the key to coronary artery disease,[4] a common complication of digestive disorders,[5] and one of the most misunderstood aspects of various prevailing recommendations concerning a healthy diet.[6]

I have described three basic facts about oils: 1. you are what you eat, 2. good oils provide for the flexibility of cell membranes, and 3. they are the raw materials for making the prostanoid hormones. I have discussed two of the three ways that dietary fats can be toxic: when they are misshapen or when they are stiff. Rancidity, the remaining way that fats can be toxic, can happen before or after they enter your body. Our taste buds (actually our sense of smell) are so sensitive to rancid changes in oils and fats that we are quite well protected from consuming oils that have gone bad in this way. The same damage that constitutes rancidity can happen after fatty acid molecules have reached their destination in our bodies. It is worth understanding the details of what happens to fatty acids when they become rancid, because once you have grasped that process you will be able to understand the most globally toxic force affecting *all* of the molecules of the body, the enemy of youth, the ally of all diseases, and the fundamental mechanism of all injury, deterioration, aging, and death: oxidation.

If oils are extracted in the old-fashioned way, without heat or chemicals, they retain many of the protective substances that keep them from going bad. Only when oils are filtered and refined to remove these protective substances and make them clear do they become subject to oxidation or what we know as rancidity. So far I have referred to the toxic properties of fats in terms of their texture—stiff or flexible. Because the texture of the fats in your body is completely dependent on the flexibility of the fats in your diet, it makes sense to favor flexible oils over stiff oils. Your palate may be quite blind to the different viscosity, saturation, stiffness, or omega factor of various oils but it is relatively acute when it comes to rancidity. So you may say, "What is the problem? I don't eat any rancid oils." Indeed, you have a built-in capacity to taste rancidity when it is present at a very dilute concentration in any oil that you eat. You may be quite blind to the big difference between mineral oil and vegetable oil but you have an acute sense of the difference between a fresh oil and one that has just begun to turn. However, as far as the body is concerned, rancidity's ill effect really occurs after you eat oils (which may taste perfectly fine) and they become part of cell membranes. Thus it is essential to good health not to allow the body's oils to become rancid.

The following illustrative skit will provide a metaphor for understanding not only what happens when fats become oxidized or rancid, but also the series of events that protect fats and all of our other living molecules from undergoing the same damage. These events are important to understanding oxidation and antioxidants, which are as important as they are complex. The complexity of antioxidants may be easier for you to keep in mind if you use your visual memory; hence the following short play is offered for you to envision.

The first character is the Juggler, who represents a fatty acid molecule with its electrons in the air. The Juggler could, however, be any molecule in the body including DNA. The second character is the

Rogue, who represents any kind of oxidative stress. The third is Ascorbia, the lady in white, playing the role of vitamin C. Other players will appear as the scene unfolds.

Imagine the Juggler in a crowd of tourists. He is magnificent, able to keep seven objects in the air, a swarm of sparkling items that shine like the sequins of his costume. It almost seems as if he is casting parts of his very self into the air as the rhythmic simplicity of his juggling captivates us and compels us to give him room in the crowd. Now there is a disruption at the edge of the onlookers as a busybody emerges and violates the space around the Juggler. It is the greedy young Rogue charging the juggler and shouting, "I want one, I want one." Enter Ascorbia, dressed in white, stepping from the crowd to intervene just as the Juggler begins to feel the pull of the Rogue's approach. "Don't take his," she cries, "take mine," and she holds out a sparkling article, which disappears in the grasp of the Rogue. The entertainment continues as the crowd offers grateful glances to Ascorbia who, however, is bereft of her sparkling article and looking sad until Bio Flavonoid, her companion dressed in yellow, offers her one just like it. She is soothed, but now Bio Flavonoid slips from the crowd with an air of dejection that is immediately broken by the bounding presence of a large golden retriever named Carrots, who lays a shimmering sphere at the feet of Bio Flavonoid and then runs off. If we were to follow Carrots, we would see her head straight for an old man named V. E. Shute with baggy pants and pockets glowing with replacements for the sparkling objects. Mr. Shute is visited regularly and replenished by a princely figure, Regie or reduced glutathione (RG), whom I described more fully in Chapter 8.

If the sparkling objects are electrons, then the Juggler, the members of the crowd, the lady, her companion, the dog, and the old man are all molecules. Let's replace the Juggler with a fatty acid molecule. The unruly Rogue could be any of several kinds of oxidative stress that have a common greed for electrons. Atmospheric oxygen is the most abundant of such electron-hungry substances. We use it to enable us to take electrons from the sugar and fat molecules we use for fuel. The disassembly of our fuel molecules is accomplished by the removal of their electrons. The need for oxygen to do this, however, threatens us with the prospect that the molecules we wish to keep intact are subject to oxygen's burning influence. Suffice it to say that it is oxygen and all related oxidative stresses that put our molecules at risk of losing an electron. Such a loss is a necessary part of all chemistry in which molecules participate voluntarily. All chemistry has to do with the sharing, gaining, or losing of electrons from one atom or molecule (a collection of atoms whose electrons swarm together).

The involuntary or inadvertent loss of electrons from molecules whose integrity is important to the structure of our cell membranes, DNA, the skin, or the clear substances in the eye results in damage or disease. The oxidative stress may be physical trauma, exposure to chemicals or heavy metals such as mercury or lead, the wear and tear of aging, or a burn, which is oxidation in its most extreme form.

The fire from a candle flame aptly illustrates oxidation in which the electrons of the candle wax are ripped off by oxygen in the atmosphere with the resulting, self-perpetuating release of light and heat. If a fatty acid molecule gets its electron ripped off by oxygen in the air, it is damaged. If the fatty acid molecule is a pat of butter or olive oil, we call the damage rancidity. If the fatty acid molecule is nested among millions of others in the velvety pile of our cell membranes, we call the damage oxidative damage or peroxidation. If one cell membrane fatty acid molecule loses its electron, its neighbors feel the suction of the loss and a collective destabilization occurs so that the whole area of the membrane becomes more easily oxidized and thus damaged, altered, misshapen, and stiffened.

Enter vitamin C, an antioxidant whose companions, the bioflavonoids, aid in the transfer of a replacement electron. Beta-carotene is a necessary bridge in the transfer of a new electron from vitamin E, which is replenished in turn by glutathione. In the end the replacements are supplied by a nutrient-rich diet. However, the path from dietary intake to antioxidant protection through the generosity of vitamin C is dependent on an inflexible sequence that is very much like a bucket brigade and it quenches a problem that is very much like a fire.

Another firefighter's instrument, a ladder, is an even better image than a bucket brigade for understanding antioxidants. It is an especially good metaphor to underline the flaws in various research efforts that cast doubt on the value or safety of particular antioxidants. A recent study[7] of vitamin E and beta-carotene in heavy smokers in Finland suggested that beta-carotene might be dangerous because of its statistical association with a higher incidence of lung cancer in men who took supplements of beta-carotene as part of a long-term experiment studying the effects of vitamin E and/or beta-carotene supplementation. The antioxidant brigade is like a ladder: it depends on the presence of all of the rungs for its safe operation. Modern scientific thinking favors experiments in which a very limited number of variables are studied while all the other circumstances are controlled. That approach translates into selecting a single drug, nutrient, or other intervention to be studied, avoiding the confusion that would result from the introduction of several variables at once.

The same question comes up every day in my practice. After taking a history and doing tests that indicate a lack of certain nutrients and/or the presence of certain allergens or toxins, I suggest that my patient undertake several remedial steps at once. These may also include advice to exercise, learn diaphragmatic breathing, meditate, or verbalize strong feelings such as anger or grief. "But how will we know what is working?" asks an occasional patient. If you get better, you may be quite confused. It is preferable to be confused and better than to be so selective that progress may be impossible. Remember that if you are sitting on two tacks and you remove just one, you will not feel 50 percent better. Chronic illness is multifactorial. It is downright negligent to focus so exclusively on a single treatment that you fail to address the whole picture.

What about the Finnish smokers? The researchers who carried out the experiment followed an understandable, but in this case, inappropriate, instinct to be selective. They chose to study only one or two antioxidants that function as members of a team of many. One, beta-carotene, becomes toxic itself if it cannot become replenished by vitamin E, which in turn, runs short if sufficient supplies of riboflavin (vitamin B_2) are not available. It is as if a study were designed to validate that ladders are useful tools for firefighters to climb to put out a fire by breaking the ladder down to its components and testing each one individually. Such a study would prove that a long ladder with many rungs missing is not only useless, but potentially dangerous. The experiment of the Finnish smokers was conducted with scientific precision. Its flaw was a fundamental ignorance of antioxidant chemistry. Antioxidants do not work alone.

Fat is arguably the most important material in the body. It is responsible for the packaging of every cell, the membranous support for most cellular activity, and the raw material for making the hormones that communicate between cells. As this picture has emerged over the past thirty years, it was a revelation to me. When I went to medical school the chemistry of fat was glossed over as dull and unimportant. It is even more surprising to me that the cholesterol frenzy of recent years has taken precedence over the significance of good fatty acids. By good fatty acids I mean not only alpha-linolenic and linoleic acids, but the avoidance of factors that introduce stiffness and flaws into the fabric of our fatty membrane acreage. Eating stiff (saturated) or altered (trans, hydrogenated) fats is a problem because the palate is absolutely no help in protecting us from the toxicity of these molecules. I reemphasize that rancid fats are a problem not because we tend to eat so much of them, but because oxidation threatens our fatty acid molecules after they are eaten and have already taken up their proper place in our membranes. Oxidative damage is a threat to nearly all molecules in our body, but the threat to fatty acids has a special twist. Remember that when they are membrane molecules, fatty acid jugglers are not alone in a crowd but are members of a continuous formation of jugglers packed together like a marching band in tight formation. Oxidative damage affects them more than other molecules in the body because of the domino effect that occurs when one of their fatty acids becomes oxidized.

There is a big molecule, superoxide dismutase, that can actually grab and subdue oxidative stress before vitamin C comes to the rescue. For the most part, however, the protection of our fatty acid membranes and other important molecules is a quintessentially cooperative enterprise in which hundreds of molecules that are not ordinarily considered antioxidants can lend a hand (or an electron) when the need arises. The failure of antioxidant protection yields a toxic effect on molecules of all kinds. The molecules that are the most precious jewels of our chemistry are the DNA that carry the instructions that maintain our identity in each of the cells as well as our ancestral identity.

Fatty Acids

What can you can do to improve your fatty acids? The stakes are enormous and the rules are simple. The stakes have to do with lowering your risk or improving your health in just about every way you can name. Stories and studies show how fatty acid supplementation can help this or that disease or condition. I hope, however, that what you have read in this chapter helps you understand that fatty acids work at such a deep layer in body chemistry that they are good for everyone, but in different degrees and different ways. Individuality is the key to most good medical treatment of chronic conditions. More than any other sphere of nutrition, fatty acids are, however, a kind of panacea in the modern world in which deficiency of omega-3 oils is nearly universal. The rules are simple: consume more omega-3 fatty acids and fewer omega-6 fatty acids. Here are some options.

OmegaBrite

OmegaBrite is a refined fish oil concentrate in a capsule. Of all the omega-3 products it is the least likely to result in fishy burps or any other side effect or adverse reaction. A dose of two to three capsules daily should suffice for maintenance, but much larger doses may be needed to provide the volume needed for an oil change in someone who has a deficit of omega-3 and an excess of bad fatty acids. OmegaBrite contains 500 mg of fatty acids per capsule with a ratio of 7:1 EPA to DHA. It is available from OmegaBrite.com.

Cod Liver Oil

How the heck did people figure out that taking the oil from the liver of a fish and giving it to kids would be a good idea? There is nothing to compare with it in the traditions of the Western world that persisted into the last century. Garlic and some herbs and spices are healthy to eat, but the oil extracted from the livers of cod fish stands alone as a product specifically chosen to fortify the children and heal various woes of our ancestors right down to my generation, which received the nasty-tasting stuff as a daily ritual until the specialty of pediatrics declared it old-fashioned, much to the relief (and peril) of children and grown-ups alike. Cod liver oil was known in ancient Egypt for its quality to heal certain kinds of blindness associated, we know now, with deficiency of vitamin A. The thread from that practice to the use of cod liver oil for children is buried in history. Contemporary products of cod liver oil should be certified to be free of mercury, polychlorinate biphenyls, and dioxins; should contain the natural form of vitamin A, not vitamin A palmitate (some people are sensitive to palmitate); and should have an acceptable flavor indicating a lack of rancidity—corresponding to laboratory certification of low levels of peroxides. One such product is available from Kirkman Laboratories (www.kirkman labs.com). One teaspoon (5 mL) contains 5,000 IU of vitamin A, 500 IU of vitamin D, 250 mg of EPA, and 250 mg of DHA. It is available in flavored and unflavored forms.

The only problem with cod liver oil is that doses of EPA and DHA needed to repair fatty acid deficits may demand doses that would lead to excessive doses of vitamins A and D. A very conservative dosage schedule for cod liver oil is ¼ teaspoon (1 mL) for babies to age two, ½ teaspoon (2.5 mL) for children from age two to five, ¾ teaspoon (3.5 mL) from age five to ten, and 1 teaspoon (5 mL) for those ten and older.

A fish oil concentrate without vitamins A and D and free of mercury, PCBs, and dioxins can be obtained from Vital Nutrients at 888-328-9992.

Flax Oil

Flax oil is about 40 percent alpha-linolenic acid, the mother of the omega-3 family of fatty acids. The next highest is walnut oil, with 10 percent. Alpha-linolenic acid is the essential fatty acid your body needs to make its own fish oils—that is the longer-chain fatty acids, EPA and DHA, which are found in OmegaBrite and cod liver oil. Most people can make their own EPA and DHA when provided with a dose of a teaspoon (5 mL) to a tablespoon (15 mL) of flax oil daily. It works beautifully to clear most of the skin symptoms of fatty acid deficiency and was put into use in the 1970s by Donald Rudin, M.D., in high doses (several tablespoons daily) for treatment of individuals with severe mental disease such as schizophrenia and mania. The only problem with flax oil arises in the occasional individual with difficulties putting alpha-linolenic acid to use as a raw material for making EPA and DHA. Such individuals have a glitch in their assembly lines for both omega-6 and omega-3 oils. Supplements of flax oil may overload the bottleneck (called delta-6-desaturase deficiency) in such individuals so that the flax oil produces undesirable effects such as worsening of allergies, hyperactivity, premenstrual tension, and some inflammatory conditions. A brief trial of flax oil is a relatively safe way to test your tolerance and no lab test is a sure predictor of success or failure. The only downside of a three- to four-week trial of flax oil would be a transient worsening or appearance of symptoms that would abate once the oil was discontinued. The value of such an adventure would be that it would point the way to the use of an omega-6 oil found in the seeds of borage, black currant, and primrose. This oil, gamma-linolenic acid (GLA), is the product of the first step in which the mother of the omega-6 family (linoleic acid) is converted to other members of the family. Compensation for the failure of that conversion (as a result of delta-6-desaturase deficiency) can be achieved by taking GLA to continue the work of the assembly line. Some all-purpose oil supplements include GLA in the formula to cover the possibility of the glitch I have just described.

Decreasing Omega-6 Oils

Except in people with delta-6-desaturase deficiency or those consuming a very low-fat diet or with inabilities to digest and absorb oils from their food, a deficit of omega-6 oils is rare. The main source of omega-6 oils in our diets is in the form of vegetable oils. Cutting down on the use of such oils while increasing your intake of omega-3 oils is the key to rebalancing your fatty acids and providing your body with the raw materials for making flexible cell membranes.

The omega-3 story is creeping onto a landscape that prevents a rapid rise in the tide of knowledge. The barriers start with a medical mind-set of my generation's scientific education that oils are dumb and continued with the subsequent generation pushing the idea that fats are bad for you while ignoring, until recently, the fact that sugars have a bigger impact on fat metabolism than fat does. Now you can begin to find sensible ways of incorporating omega-3 oils into your diet without taking supplements. Many markets now carry The Country Hen eggs, which were the first to come from free-range hens fed high omega-3 feed, which produces high omega-3 eggs. On the other hand, the most sensible way of introducing fish oils into your diet, eating more seafood, carries the risk of mercury overload. I enjoy eating some small fish, have stopped eating big fish, don't bother with farm-raised fish (their feed and oils are more like those of cattle), and get my omega-3s from a fish oil concentrate.

Here are a few rules to summarize the points I have covered in this book:

1. Keep your membranes flexible. Take a supplement of omega-3 fatty acids on a regular basis and avoid the stiff fats found in hydrogenated oils and saturated fats.

2. Hang onto your electrons. Even if you are able to eat a high-fiber, varied diet rich in fresh vegetables and fruit and lacking in sugar, you may consider taking a supplement containing the main antioxidant nutrients and their supporting cast: vitamin C, vitamin E, carotenes, selenium, zinc, and the B vitamins. Take a generous supplement of folic acid. Avoid exposure to oxidative stress such as sunburn and radiation. Supplementation with reduced glutathione is controversial because it does not appear to be absorbed when taken orally. Its observed benefits when taken by mouth may be explained by its use in the digestive tract, which spares its use in nondigestive tissues.

3. Keep your sanitation budget as low as possible by avoiding exposure to toxins, particularly heavy metals, pesticides, and petrochemicals.

4. If you need to take antibiotics, take steps to repair your bowel flora during and after the treatment.

11

Some Final Thoughts

WHEN I SEE a person who is well and wants advice on how to stay well, my checklist is pretty much the same as when I see a person who is sick and wants to get better. I think of the biggest and busiest jobs in the patient's physiologic economy. From that overall perspective I have to see each person as an individual and read his or her symptoms, physical signs, and laboratory test results to get a map of his or her unique physical and spiritual landscape. I heed the words of Oliver Sacks in his advice to a newly qualified physician: "Listen, listen minutely to every patient. Refrain from hasty judgment. See every patient as unique. See their condition from their perspective." I become a tailor trying to fit recommendations for each person.

So it is a different task to guide you with only the knowledge that you are a person who has turned the pages I have written and knows some of my story and wants to know what I think is the bottom line while acknowledging that I don't know your story. Keep in mind that among all living things there exists a strong urge and capacity to heal. The following list may guide you in that direction.

1. The medical application of systems theory says that all approachable sources of imbalance should be addressed to promote healing.

2. Correcting imbalance means getting the right amount of vitamins, minerals, fatty acids, amino acids, accessory nutritional factors, light, and love and avoiding toxins and allergens.

3. The "right amount" of positive factors and the tolerable amount of toxins and allergens vary from person to person.

4. Personal health efforts to solve problems differ from public health efforts because the former assumes that each of us is different whereas the latter assumes that we are all the same.

5. Your similarities to other people are the basis for making a diagnosis, but the differences between you and others may be the basis for guiding treatment.

6. Treatment should restore function in as many ways as possible and should resort to suppression of symptoms with drugs only as a last resort.

7. One of the body's most important functions is the elimination of unwanted used molecules and toxins that come in from the outside world.

8. Getting rid of used molecules such as hormones and neurotransmitters uses the same detoxification chemistry as does the elimination of toxins from the outside world. The only difference is that when reduced glutathione is used as an usher for the former, it is recycled, but when it binds with the latter xenobiotics, it is lost from the body.

9. Detoxification is a synthetic process in which a new molecule is made from a substance to be cleared, joined to a carrier needed to usher it safely from the body.

10. The metabolic cost of synthesizing molecules for detoxification exceeds all other processes except that of growth in children.

11. Most of the cells that make up your body are transients with a life span of a few days to a few years. A minority of cells is permanent and constitutes the basis for the persistence of your self.

12. Your immune and central nervous systems are the home of your permanent cells, which deserve especially good care.

13. Good care of your permanent cells means feeding them the right nutrients and avoiding the accumulation of toxins.

14. The surface of each cell is its protective shield and the interface by which it communicates with other cells. That surface, as well as the work surfaces for all the internal chemistry of the cells, is made of fatty acids. The health of these surfaces is maintained by a good supply of omega-3 fatty acids and protection from oxidation.

15. When you eat fat, it is not digested in the same way other nutrients are and passed through your liver. Instead it is absorbed nearly intact and passed directly into your bloodstream.

16. Your body is relatively indiscriminate when it comes to the use of fats provided in your diet, so that in terms of the composition of your body fat, you very much *are* what you eat.

17. Your body can only be so discriminating when it comes to other molecules that enter it; some of the trickiest problems in toxicity come from look-alike molecules that create mischief by their close resemblance to minerals (as does lead), neurotransmitters (as do peptides), and intermediates in energy metabolism (as do microbial organic acids).

About twenty years ago a man came to me with a multiple-allergy problem. I had asked him to fill out a complete questionnaire, and I had interviewed him at length before doing a physical exam, during which I was surprised to find a long surgical scar on his scalp. "Oh yeah," said he. "I forgot to mention that I had that operation." What operation? Removal of a brain tumor. "Oh, some sort of benign growth?" "Nope, it was a cancer that spread from my lung." "You mean to say that you had lung cancer and it spread to your brain." "Yup. First they took out the cancer from my lung and later they found it in my brain and took it out." A long scar on his chest revealed itself to my astonished eyes as I asked, "So what did they say about it?" "They just said stop smoking and don't worry. So I stopped smoking and I didn't worry." I guess you would have to say that he was an exception to the most important rule I have learned from people who have beaten the odds. People with enduring or mortal threats to their health do best when they are able to change. I have read and listened to many discussions in which the issue of compliance is raised by physicians who are skeptical of the role of diet, nutrition, exercise, meditation, coping with loss, and other aspects of what has become known as lifestyle. "When people are sick they have a hard enough time just taking their medicine. All that other stuff just uses up their energy so they are less likely to focus on taking their pills."

It may be true that the "average person" just wants to take a pill and not be bothered by making changes. It may also be true that such a person has a hard time making the distinction between what is appropriate for an acute versus a chronic illness. If so, then the message of this book goes beyond the several key points and has to do with change.

The changes I have in mind differ from person to person. For some it means a new job, for others a new spiritual orientation, and for others learning better ways of loving and being loved. For many it means a change in biochemistry, the subject I have addressed in this book. Those who can face choices without ambivalence do better than others. The ones who do best are the ones who realize that they have been sitting on a need to change and understand the underlying message of this book: illness is a signal to change.

Notes

Preface

1. Smithells, R.W.; Sheppard, S.; and Schorah, C. J. Vitamin deficiencies and neural tube defects. *Arch Dis Child*, 1976; Dec. 51(12):944–50.

Chapter 3

1. Williams, R. J. *Biochemical Individuality: The Basis for the Genetotrophic Concept*. New York: Wiley, 1956.
2. Stejskal, J. S., et al. Immunologic and brain MRI changes in patients with suspected metal intoxication. *Intl J Occup Med Toxicol*, 1955; 4:1–9.
3. Stejskal, F. D. M., et al. MELISA, an *in vitro* tool for the study of metal allergy. *Toxic in vitro*, 1994; 8:991–1000.
4. Black, D.W.; Rutha, A.; and Goldstein, R. B. Environmental illness: a controlled study of 26 subjects with "20th century disease." *JAMA*, 1990; 264:3166–70.
5. Ashford, N., and Miller, C. *Chemical Exposures: Low Levels, High Stakes*. New York: Van Nostrand, 1991.

6. Memorandum for All Regional Counsel from George L. Weidenfeller, Deputy General Counsel, U.S. Department of Housing and Urban Development, April 11, 1992. Subject: Multiple Chemical Sensitivity Disorder and Environmental Illness as Handicaps.

7. See: *Warmoth v. Bowen*, No. 85–2835 United States Court of Appeals, Seventh Circuit [798 F.2d 1109 (7th Cir. 1986)] and *Kouril v. Bowen*, No. 89–5187MN United States Court of Appeals, Eighth Circuit [912 F.2d 971 (8th Cir. 1990)].

8. Rea, W. *Chemical Sensitivity,* vols. I–IV. Boca Raton, FL: CRC Press.

9. Rogers, S. *Wellness at All Odds.* Syracuse, NY: Prestige Publishing, 1994. This is Dr. Rogers's most recent work and it cites her many other books and articles containing information and advice for patients.

10. Jefferies, W. M. *Safe Uses of Cortisone.* Springfield, IL: Charles C. Thomas, 1981.

11. Ibid.

Chapter 4

1. Campbell, D. G. The ordeal of poor old Charlie, "drunkless drunk." Los Angeles Times News Service, January 1983.

2. Crook, W. *The Yeast Connection.* Jackson, TN: Professional Books, 1986.

3. Truss, O. *The Missing Diagnosis.* P.O. Box 26508, Birmingham, AL, 1982.

4. Coulter, H. L. *Divided Legacy*, 2d ed. Richmond, CA: North Atlantic Books, 1982.

5. Shaw, W.; Chaves, E.; and Luxem, M. Abnormal urine organic acids associated with fungal metabolism in urine samples of children with autism: preliminary results of a clinical trial with antifungal drugs. *Proc of the National Autism Society of America*, July 1995.

6. Werbach, M. R. *Nutritional Influences on Illness*. New Canaan, CT: Keats Publishing, Inc., 1988.
7. Adlercreutz, H. Lignans and isoflavonoids and their possible role in prevention of cancer. Paper presented at The Third International Symposium on Functional Medicine, Vancouver, British Columbia, March 1996.

Chapter 6

1. Deth, R. *Molecular Origins of Human Attention: The Dopamine-Folate Connection*. Boston: Kluwer, 2003, p. 185.
2. The toxicological effects of methyl mercury, National Research Council of the National Academy of Sciences, National Academy Press, Washington, D.C., 2001.
3. Carson, B. L.; Ellis, H. V.; and McCann, T. L. *Toxicology and Biological Monitoring of Metals in Humans*. Chelsea, MI: Lewis Publishers, 1986.

Chapter 8

1. Baker, S. M. *Folic Acid*. New Canaan, CT: Keats Publishing, Inc., 1995.
2. McCully, K. S. Vascular pathology of homocysteinuria: implications for the pathogenesis of arteriosclerosis. *Am J Pathol*, 1969; 56:111–28.
3. Stamler, J. S., and Slivka, A. Biological chemistry of thiols in the vasculature and in vascular-related disease. *Nutrition Reviews*, 1996; 54:1–30.
4. Clarke, R.; Daly, L.; and Robinson, K., et al. Hyperhomocysteine: an independent factor for vascular disease. *N Eng J Med*, 1991; 324:1149–55.
5. Baker, S. M. *Folic Acid*. New Canaan, CT: Keats Publishing, Inc., 1995.

Chapter 9

1. Bower, L. P. Ecological chemistry. *Scientific American*, 1969; 220:2, 22–29.
2. Husemann, F., and Wolff, O. *The Anthroposophical Approach to Medicine*, vol. II. Hudson, NY: Anthroposophic Press, 1987, p. 125.
3. Bland, J. Oxidants and antioxidants in clinical medicine: past, present and future. *J Nutr and Environ Med*, 1995; 5:255–80.

Chapter 10

1. MetaMetrix Laboratory, 5000 Peachtree Industrial Boulevard, Norcross, GA 30011, 800-221-4640; and Great Smokies Diagnostic Laboratory, 800-522-4762.
2. Siguel, E., M.D., Ph.D. P.O. Box 5, Brookline, MA 02146-0001. E-mail: nutrek@efafood.com. Website: www.efafood.com.
3. ———. *Essential Fatty Acids in Health and Disease*. Brookline, MA: Nutrek Press, 1994. (Nutrek Press, P.O. Box 1269, Brookline, MA 02146).
4. Siguel, E., and Lerman, R. H. Fatty acid patterns in patients with angiographically documented coronary artery disease. *Metabolism*, 1994; 43:982–93.
5. ———. Fatty acid patterns in patients with chronic intestinal disease. *Metabolism*, 1996; 45(1):12–23.
6. Additional fatty acid references:
   Siguel, E., and Lerman, R. H. The effect of low-fat diet on lipid levels. *JAMA*, 1996; 275:759.
   Siguel, E. Dietary sources of long-chain n-3 polyunsaturated fatty acids. *JAMA*, 1996; 275:836.
   Siguel, E.; Lerman, R. H.; and MacBeath, B. Low-fat diets for coronary heart disease: perhaps, but which one? *JAMA*, 1996; 275:1402–3.
7. Smigel, K. Beta carotene fails to prevent cancer in two major studies, CARET intervention stopped. *J Natl Cancer Inst*, 1996; 88(3–4):145.

Index